the Christmas TV Companion

To Ron —

Have a Holly
Jolly Christmas!

Joanna [illegible]

the Christmas TV Companion

a Guide to Cult Classics, Strange Specials & Outrageous Oddities

by Joanna Wilson

1701 Press
Akron, Ohio

Proudly published by 1701 Press, Cuyahoga Falls, Ohio
www.1701press.com

Printed and Bound in the United States of America
First Printing 2010

ISBN 978-0-9842699-4-5

Design by Dominic Caruso
http://domcaruso.com

Icon Legend

Hidden Gems

Kids' Christmas

Make Your Own Marathon

Table of Contents

Acknowledgements

I AM GREATLY INDEBTED TO THE PEOPLE who supported and encouraged me throughout this project. The following individuals have contributed their time to the preparation of this book and my appreciation can not be overstated: Steve Wolcott, Stephanie Burley, Kendra Minadeo (www.KLMfilms.com), Jill Grimm (www.jillgrimmnow.com), Stuart Morgan Kunkle, Michael D. Toth (luxuriamusic.com/djprofiles/tothar) and Kiki Howell (www.kikihowell.com).

Thanks to everyone at 1701 Press. And, of course, my deepest appreciation goes to my loving and patient partner who graciously lets me control the DVD player with the television volume on full blast with Christmas episodes throughout the whole year.

Get Ready For the Weirdest Christmas Ever, An Introduction

Christmas on TV is out there. I mean, way out there. A show about hillbilly squids that kidnap Santa Claus? It's been done. What about a show starring both David Bowie and Bing Crosby singing a Christmas duet? Yeah, it happened. How about an alternate version of Santa as a gift-bearing hog—or a kids' show that imagines the devastating results of a vampire Santa? They've been produced too. Post-apocalyptic Christmas, Christmas on the moon, Christmas on Mars. Like I said, television's Christmases are out there—crazy, profane, innovative, cheesy and classic. I've seen it and I'm here to share it all with you.

Why write a book about cult Christmas TV classics? Initially, it seemed like a narrow focus for a book, but I quickly found more surprises than I was expecting. Television itself continues to splinter into more new networks that are attempting to reach ever-narrowing demographics and niche markets. We as viewers have changed, demanding more and more attention-grabbing programming to suit our tastes. So too, this book may appeal to an audience of television specialists: active television viewers. I'm not talking about casual viewers who are just interested in the newest programs, but those who have developed a taste for what they like and have strong opinions about it. These viewers take unrepentant joy in watching television, often watching things over and over, paying attention to the details of character, dialogue and theme. Just as these viewers are devoted to watching TV more intensively, they will be interested in watching Christmas programming that goes beyond the ordinary.

Christmas material has its own cult-like status. Most holiday programming airs only once a year, so it has a built-in value because of its rarity. The shows are also filled with heightened emotions, from nostalgia and sentimentality to optimism and innocence. We tend to bond to these emotional programs as children, no matter how sappy or poor in quality. We still love to watch them well into our adult lives and defend them as worthy of attention and respectability. While we may acknowledge that the silly sitcoms of our youth don't stand up to our adult tastes, our loyalty to Christmas television memories from our youth remains strong. Popular culture is a common language that connects and bonds us, despite the diversity of our own family holiday traditions.

In writing this book, I'm looking to appeal to those other TV addicts—you know who you are—who want to read about Christmas material they've perhaps never seen before, or reconnect with something they haven't seen since childhood. I've also included commentary on rare tidbits from the past that deserve a second look. This book may also appeal to others, who already spend time watching their favorite Christmas installments, and may be looking to expand their current repertoire.

A loyal TV junky from my earliest years, I was one of those kids whose favorite babysitter was 1970s television.

Imagine my excitement when I was cast in my second grade holiday pageant as Peppermint Patty in *A Charlie Brown Christmas.* I still have the script that two teachers from my elementary school transcribed from the animated TV special and adapted into a stage production. Although I had only two lines, the experience personally connected me to the TV special—never mind that the character of Peppermint Patty doesn't even make an appearance in the original animated classic. Perhaps because of this small detail, I've had a life-long obsession with paying attention to the details while watching TV and film. In college, I earned a degree in film and an advanced degree in philosophy, combining my love of motion pictures with analysis and evaluation. Then, in the late 1990s, I happened to receive Rick Goldschmidt's book *The Enchanted World of Rankin/Bass* as a gift. After reading it, I set myself the goal of re-watching all the Rankin/Bass Christmas specials, a project which quickly expanded into watching all the Rankin/Bass animated works. And, as I combed through my local video rental stores and library shelves, I began to find other, more obscure holiday animated programs and forgotten Christmas specials.

My hobby of watching TV Christmas specials soon became a much larger project: an encyclopedia of all things Christmas on television, including every special, holiday-themed episode and made-for-TV movie. I'm almost embarrassed to admit how long I've been watching and collecting the information for the research project I'm intending to release as a book. And I fear I've become "that strange lady"—instead of "that thorough and diligent researcher"—who is frequently spotted at the library checking out an armload of Christmas-themed videos even in July. But I can't set aside my obsession: despite several thousand entries, I'm still fascinated and frequently surprised by the diversity of the creativity that goes into the holiday material that is produced each year. There's a wide spectrum of Christmas material and it spans the best and the worst of television—from high art productions of the classical ballet, *The Nutcracker,* to the most cheaply produced, derivative children's special.

It is from the larger project of my more comprehensive Christmas encyclopedia that I have derived this book. As I have researched the history of television, combing through books, DVD sets and the Internet for Christmas titles, I love finding the rare, overlooked or forgotten installments. For my own personal tastes, I prefer the unexpected, weird, bizarre and off-center stories produced for the mass medium's audiences.

In our culture, Christmas has a very particular mythos. For example, a fairly rigid set of expectations governs what Santa can and cannot do. The rules extend to what he looks like, how he behaves, how he speaks, and so on. Christmas narratives often follow an equally rigid set of constraints. There is always a search for the true meaning of Christmas and miracles are common. The traditional themes that go into Christmas have become tightly interwoven with the holiday's sacredness, and people get uncomfortable or even angry when they are tampered with. The vast majority of Christmas material on television conforms to the conventional rules governing Christmas stories—which is not to say that these programs are uninteresting or of poor quality. Yet I'm continually surprised when the mass medium of TV offers me something new within these constraints. It's also fascinating when the rules are reinterpreted or downright ignored. This book is filled with the atypical instances of when these rules are challenged or transgressed. For example, after watching what feels like my millionth adaptation of Dickens' *A Christmas Carol,* I'll numbly watch another only to come alive again when the King of Macabre, Vincent Price appears as the story's narrator. Or, after seeing countless jolly, red-suited, rotund, elderly Santas, I'll get thrown a curve ball like the Japanese anime, *My Santa,* in which the Gift-Bringer is portrayed as a buxom, teenage girl.

What's In This Book

I've tried to limit my discussion to TV episodes, made-for-TV movies, shorts and feature-length theater releases, and specials that are available to watch. Therefore, most are accessible on DVD. Some can be viewed online, and a few are only available on VHS, but will hopefully be in a digital format soon. In my experience, the status of accessibility is always changing, something difficult to find today often becomes widely available tomorrow.

There are five chapters appealing to genres or categories on themes popular with cult TV viewers. I chose the categories specifically because of the abundance of interesting and varied Christmas material in each. Variety and Animation as categories are both television institutions with a goldmine of boundary-pushing and extraordinary Christmas programs. The Macabre and Sci-Fi chapters were chosen because each genre seems to have a loyal following that may be eager to consider Christmas installments. The final chapter which focuses on Dark-themed Christmas installments is a collection of materials from across the genres, with elements that seem antithetical to a traditional Christmas. I painstakingly selected the entries within each chapter, though there are many more possibilities. This is certainly not a complete listing of atypical

Christmas material within each genre or category. But it is a collection of the programs that stand out the most.

The first chapter covers scary or macabre holiday material, eventually including horror. A scary ghost story seems to be fitting for the Christmas season, whether it's Charles Dickens' one or a more contemporary tale. Look for your favorite Vincent Price holiday moment or the most noteworthy ax-wielding Santa Claus movie. The second chapter includes a discussion of the most interesting science fiction holiday installments spanning material adapted from celebrated sci-fi authors, such as Arthur C. Clarke, to comedy episodes about alien visitors from space and their first Christmas experiences. The third chapter concerns itself with television's most unusual and off-center moments in the variety genre, musical performances by unexpected guests as well as the best recent productions. The fourth chapter covers outrageous Christmas-themed animation created for television, including take-offs of everybody's favorite cartoon classics, Rankin/Bass' *Rudolph, A Charlie Brown Christmas* and *How the Grinch Stole Christmas!*, as well as a careful consideration of the most off-the-wall of Cartoon Network's Adult Swim holiday programs. And, the final chapter covers a grab-bag of material that is considered dark, odd or quirky for holiday-themed television programming. This covers post-apocalyptic visions of Christmas and movies with inappropriate or atypical Christmas scenes—including a John Waters' movie and an unusual *film noir*.

Within each chapter are three additional subsections: Hidden Gems, Kids' Christmas and Make Your Own Marathon.

Hidden Gems

The Hidden Gems are comprised of holiday material

that is non-mainstream, overlooked or underappreciated and deserving of a second viewing.

Kids' Christmas

Kids' Christmas is a suggestion for child-appropriate or more family-friendly installments in keeping with the theme of each chapter. Please note: some of the entries in this book are recommended for mature viewers or parental guidance is suggested. I advise parents to check with the individual recommended ratings for each program before watching. However, it is my opinion that all the Kids' Christmas listings are appropriate for young viewers. I made the additional effort to select rich enough installments so that most are still interesting for adult viewers as well.

Make Your Own Marathon

The Make Your Own Marathon (MYOM) listings are practical suggestions to help you construct your own schedule of holiday material. Take control of your celebrations by finding this material at your local library, in your online rental queue, by setting your DVR, or by purchasing your favorite holiday DVDs to construct the Christmas experience that you want. How many times in the past has it felt less than Christmas because you missed your favorite Christmas special or weren't able to find it airing? Hopefully, with this *Companion*, you can have the holiday that feels right for you. If there's one thing I've learned from watching television—it's that every family's traditions and values are unique and meaningful to them. So why can't your sci-fi Christmas or horror-filled holiday be as meaningful too?

Additionally, between each chapter are four longer MYOM suggestions. The first is a list of the coolest stars in our culture and their appearance in or connection to

Christmas material. Aren't you just dying to know where you can watch Steve McQueen or Sinatra's Rat Pack celebrating Christmas? There is also a list of twelve cult TV series and the Christmas episodes of these programs. These twelve are not intended as a complete listing of cult TV programs. This list is provided as a way to add more Christmas installments of your favorite cult TV shows that are not already mentioned within the chapters. Thirdly, there is a listing of overlooked Christmas specials that could use a fresh viewing. These Second Chance specials may not only bring back fond memories for some, but inspire new devotees.

And finally in the appendix, I've included instructions on how to make your own Make Your Own Marathon. There you will find an example of a MYOM to guide you of the 1998 cult film, *The Big Lebowski*. I've chosen *The Big Lebowski* as a model because it is one of the more popular and visible cult film phenomena of the last ten years. It has a large devoted following with numerous fan gatherings around the world each year at which the details and minutia of the movie are re-lived and expanded beyond the film itself. Fans of the film can use this MYOM to watch their favorite *Lebowski* stars in Christmas material. But of course, the instructions on how to make your own will allow you to find Christmas programming related to a film of your own choosing.

No summary in this book is an adequate substitute for watching the original material itself. My only intent is to provide some framework and description to help you choose what to watch, or perhaps challenge you to re-watch something from a new perspective. Hopefully, there are a few things in here that are already your favorites as well as a few surprises. Okay, TV fans, make your's a Merry Christmas.

Have Yourself an Eerie Little Christmas

In *A Christmas Carol,* author Charles Dickens understood the psychological ramifications of emotions running high during the holidays and of fear being the most intense connection for his readers. His work continues to inspire us to share thrilling ghost stories with family and friends. It seems appropriate that we enjoy scaring ourselves during what is literally the darkest time of the year. Dickens' most famous Christmas story breathed life into four ghosts and there have been holiday scary stories ever since. Perhaps it's a sign of modern society that we take joy in heightening our fears during the same seasonal period that our ancient ancestors were most concerned with surviving the longest night of the year.

Some of us like to feel the creepy atmosphere usually associated with Halloween at Christmas time as well. A dark favorite is *Tim Burton's The Nightmare Before Christmas,* the 1993 feature length animated film. Jack Skellington, the Pumpkin King of Halloween Town, craves the challenge and excitement of experiencing something new so he decides to take over the role of Santa Claus from Christmas Town. But, when Jack brings his own frighteningly dark vision to the children of the world, he finds he only disappoints and terrorizes instead of bringing them the joy of Christmas. This visually stunning, delightful story contains more than just a skeleton in a Santa suit; there is also Oogie Boogie, the boogeyman, a rag doll stitched together like Frankenstein's creature, a mad scientist, as well as an assortment of ghouls, ghosts and odd monsters.

Infamous weirdo, the boogeyman, shows up in several adaptations of the Christmas favorite, ***Babes in Toyland****, as well as in* ***The Nightmare Before Christmas****.*

Cue Sinister Laughter

Who's more eerie than the Master of the Macabre himself? Vincent Price brings a thrilling atmosphere to Christmas better than anyone. Worth seeking out is the nearly forgotten, 1949 made-for-TV special, *Charles Dickens' The Christmas Carol.* In chilling black-and-white, Price serves as the classic story's narrator, appearing between dramatic segments sitting in a chair as if reading the story to the audience.

What is Dr. Seuss' Grinch if not a green, furry monster? His monstrousness is reinforced when the creature's story is narrated by legendary monster movie actor Boris Karloff. Extending this layer of meaning, actor Anthony Hopkins, well-known for his role as man-eater, Hannibal Lecter, provided narration in the live action version from 2000.

Price also provides his distinctive voice for one of the two heads of the Troll King in the animated children's program, 1987's *The Little Troll Prince.* This religious-themed Christmas TV special explains how a troll prince with no desire to follow in his father's wicked footsteps escapes to the human world. There, he learns about God's message, and goes on to become an adorable, pleasant little gnome. Vincent Price's final screen performance was an appearance in Tim Burton's 1990 film, *Edward Scissorhands.* He plays the role of the Inventor who dies tragically before he can give his creation, Edward, flesh for hands. The movie's story climaxes on the holiday with the neighbors avoiding the Boggs' family Christmas party and eventually chasing Edward back into the isolated mansion on the hill. This fairy tale of a movie, told by Hollywood's favorite dark storyteller Tim Burton is a heartwarming film with a romantic gothic edge.

Quoth the Raven, "Nevermore"

Northern Exposure's third season, holiday episode entitled "Seoul Mates" provides an intriguing mix of Christmas cheer and spookiness. The custom of Cicely, Alaska's residents is to celebrate the holiday incorporating the folklore of the Native Americans, honoring a mythological story about a raven. The town is covered in black bird decorations and lights. Dr. Fleischman's soft spoken secretary, Marilyn, is cast in the lead role of the town's raven pageant, and Chris' morning radio show includes Edgar Allan Poe-inspired commentary about the creepy bird we usually associate with darker sentiments. The Emmy award-winning episode creatively includes the local mythology of the raven, which metaphorically resembles the familiar Nativity story, with an emphasis on the themes of birth and light.

When Santa Attacks

If you think about it, we commonly share stories with our children that could easily have a sinister tone: a supernatural old man, dressed in a red and white suit made of animal fur, who assisted by his minions of elves breaks into our homes each Christmas Eve to dispense rewards or punishment based on an ambiguous notion of what's nice or naughty—after voyeuristically observing us all through the year. Aren't we inviting nightmares from the frightening images inherent in our cultivation of the holiday?

If this sort of twisted fear makes your heart race, you may enjoy watching the 1989 episode "And All Through the House" from the TV series, *Tales From the Crypt*. This campy installment features an unfaithful wife who brutally murders her husband on Christmas Eve with the intention of blaming it on a killer she hears a warning about from the radio. Unfortunately, the scales of justice are not tipping in her favor when the ax-wielding escapee from the local asylum, now dressed in a Santa Claus suit, comes to her house and wants in! Completists shouldn't miss the British made, 1972 Amicus Productions feature film, *Tales From the Crypt*. The film's first segment, starring grand dame Joan Collins, is from the same original story. Both segments were inspired by the popular horror comic.

Photo: *Joan Collins and Oliver MacGreevey going toe-to-toe in* ***Tales From the Crypt*** *(1972).*

Cinerama Releasing Corporation/ Photofest

The bizarre British TV comedy series, *The League of Gentlemen* brilliantly created their Christmas Special in 2000, entitled "Yule Never Leave," which takes its inspiration from anthology horror films, like the above Amicus Productions, to make one of the most unusual holiday shows ever. These funny men weave three vignettes into one story, as the characters from the small village of Royston Vasey confide in the vicar on Christmas Eve. The

placed prominently on the shelves of every video rental store and online rental queue, horror feature length options include gory, vintage slashers more appropriate for adults as well as more accessible, crass, campy comedies.

Campy Christmas

The ever popular, *Gremlins,* originally released in theaters in 1984, featured a campy fear fest about the out-of-control yet adorable mogwai. The man who brings one home from the mysterious Chinese shop for his son as a Christmas present doesn't anticipate the consequences of ignoring the three rules given to him for the care of these ultimate exotic pets. This is the classic cautionary tale about not taking proper responsibility for your Christmas gifts.

Don't confuse 1996's *Jack Frost* with the Michael Keaton holiday film of the same title. This *Jack Frost* is the outlandish story of a serial killer who is mutated by a genetically engineered substance and transformed into a murderous giant snowman on a killing spree. If that's not enough campy fun, find its even lower budget sequel: *Jack Frost 2: Revenge of the Mutant Killer*. Here, the slaying snowman follows his arch-nemesis to the Caribbean to exact his revenge at Christmas. I dare you not to laugh!

A more contemporary campy classic is 2006's *Santa's Slay,* starring professional wrestler David Goldberg as Santa Claus. Nordic legend reveals that Santa is actually the son of Satan, who lost a bet to a clever angel and was forced to spend a thousand years being kind and generous handing out gifts to children annually. But, now that Santa's thousand year curse is lifted, he's back to being the hell-raising, slayer that goes on a killing spree targeting both the naughty and the nice. Angel's grandson, Nicholas Yuleson takes up the responsibility for stopping him. Don't miss the star-studded opening sequence of the squabbling family at Christmas dinner featuring James Caan, Fran Drescher, Chris Kattan and Rebecca Gayheart.

A particular favorite is 2003's *Dead End,* starring Ray Wise as the family patriarch. The bickering Harrington family takes a short cut while on the road to grandma's house on Christmas Eve. As the seemingly endless route leads them no closer to their destination, they encounter a spooky woman who drifts out from the woods and a sinister vehicle on this road to nowhere with gruesome passengers. Thus begins a nightmarish journey filled with terror, emotional confessions, mental breakdowns and death. This horror with a lot of black humor has a twist at the end, leaving viewers with the experience of an extended episode of *The Twilight Zone* or even a vintage horror film, despite its relatively contemporary release date. This film will leave even the most dysfunctional families rethinking their petty fights in the car on Christmas Eve!

Actor, Ray Wise, the lead in ***Dead End*** *is also well remembered as the actor who played Leland Palmer in the creepy TV enigma,* ***Twin Peaks****.*

Ho-ho-horror!

Director Bob Clark did more to permanently associate his name with Christmas films than create the now-classic *A Christmas Story*. He also blazed a trail with his brilliantly made 1974 cult slasher flick, *Black Christmas*. The story takes place in a sorority house at Christmas time as female residents begin to disappear and obscene phone calls are received by the remaining house mates who are unaware that the deadly danger is lurking in the house with them.

The thrill in watching *Black Christmas* today is in the rarely imitated, open ended conclusion of the story. The film ends before the killer is caught! This terrifying lack of completion also means viewers are left to speculate just who is this serial killer and why he does what he does—

making the imagined far more scary than the usual tying up of loose story ends with the complete explanation provided in most other horror films. There is speculation amongst this film's fans concerning its legacy and the extent of influence this film has had on the slasher genre. Many claim it as the inspiration for 1978's better remembered *Halloween* and its tremendous success.

The influence of *Black Christmas* was strong enough to inspire a 2006 remake. This updated and bloodier version of the story removes the mystery behind the supposed killer, the no longer unseen, Billy. Here, the character of the criminally insane Billy is expanded and explained, and he's not working alone! There's also an update on the story line with the obscene phone calls. In this remake, cell phones reveal the origin of the calls, and ring tones sound off the location of the caller within the house. Whimsically, it recasts actress, Andrea Martin, also from the original film, now playing the more age-appropriate house mother instead of a sorority sister.

*It is also fun to watch **Black Christmas** (1974) for its recognizable cast of stars: Margot Kidder went on to star as Lois Lane in 1978's **Superman**; Olivia Hussey played Juliet, in director Franco Zeffirelli's 1968 film, **Romeo and Juliet**; Andrea Martin is one of the stars of the Canadian satire series, **SCTV**; and Keir Dullea, who plays the boyfriend Peter, also appeared in the lead role in Stanley Kubrick's masterpiece, **2001: A Space Odyssey**.*

1980's *Christmas Evil* was the first horror film to feature Santa Claus as a gruesome killer, though it was not a typical teen slasher film. Instead, we're given a much more subtle story of a man's slow descent into madness as he embodies the hero he's been obsessed with since childhood, Santa Claus. The emotionally unbalanced, toy factory worker, Harry Stadling, decides to embody the myth of Santa, someone our culture has imbued with the privilege of handing out justice: to reward the "nice" and punish the "naughty." At Christmas time, Harry becomes fed up with the morally ambiguous ethics applied to adults, i.e.: a coworker that takes advantage of his friends and a boss who makes empty promises to donate toys to a children's hospital. Thus, he begins to mete out the justice we expect from a morally unambiguous Santa Claus. Check out the ending: Santa/Harry is chased by the torch-wielding neighbors and his sleigh-painted truck drives off the cliff—Harry escapes punishment for his "crimes" by floating up into the sky as if pulled by his flying reindeer up to the heavens where we can expect to see him again next year!

This was the first killer Santa movie released in theaters, but it largely went unnoticed, probably for its more subtle plot. Though several adults are viciously killed in the film, Santa is still every child's friend; and he's protected by children in several scenes—making it even creepier. The fun of this movie is it expects viewers to rethink our own ethical behavior and hypocrisy in relation to the black-and-white ethics we claim to embrace at Christmas. Or, face the ultimate justice of Santa Claus!

1984's *Silent Night, Deadly Night* featured a Santa Claus killer who attracted the first real protests from parents' groups to remove the film from theaters. Although this slasher is pretty tame by today's standards, it's sometimes nice to return to the classics. Film critics panned it as trash, but this controversial classic has gone on to inspire four sequels and countless other tasteless Christmas releases.

In *Silent Night, Deadly Night,* a young boy named Billy watches as his mother and father are murdered by a man dressed as Santa Claus. Growing up in a religious orphanage, his trauma is only met with punishment and repression. Now as an adult, Billy works as a toy store clerk until he's forced to fill-in as the store's Santa Claus. His past trauma is triggered when he sees a coworker attacked in the stock room after the staff Christmas party and Billy, still in his costume, goes on a killing rampage. The serial killer now roams the town with an ax, punishing who he judges as naughty—in the conventions of a slasher film, these are often topless teenage girls. My favorite scenes feature a headless sledder and a nun imploring, "There's no such thing as Santa Claus" while the deranged Santa stands over her with his ax raised.

For a twist on the killer Santa plot, watch the 1984 film, *Don't Open Till Christmas.* In this British horror film, a masked madman is slicing up Santa Clauses on the streets of London at Christmas time—a departure from the typical Santa slayer. An interfering news reporter and the daughter of one of the Santa victims each launch their own investigation making Scotland Yard's Inspector Harris come under scrutiny as a suspect. It's unsurprising that the homicidal maniac ends up being a former asylum patient, and the plot certainly has its other weaknesses. However, watching Santa after Santa getting butchered, castrated or slashed can really put one in the holiday mood! Don't

__Photo__: Robert Brian Wilson as a Santa with an axe to grind in __Silent Night, Deadly Night__ (1984).

TriStar Pictures/ Photofest

miss the final scenes of the movie: even after the lunatic is caught, he gets his last vengeance with a present marked "Don't Open Till Christmas!"

MYOM:
Santa: Portrait of a Serial Killer

If none of this horror strikes your fancy, you may want to generate your own Christmas marathon, gathering together the actors who originally portrayed your favorite serial killing monsters from previous classic movies. Christmas just isn't the holiday unless you spend it with those you love.

Actor, Ted Levine, known for his iconic role as Buffalo Bill/Jame Gumb in the 1991 classic, *The Silence of the Lambs,* also appears on the long running TV series *Monk,* playing police captain Leland Stottlemeyer. Look for the 2005 episode, "Mr. Monk and the Secret Santa" which features a story about Stottlemeyer as his office secret Santa gift of a bottle of wine turns out to be poisoned. Wait for the scene with Captain Stottlemeyer singing "O Holy Night" at the office Christmas party with his goofy assistant, Randy, providing the harmony.

Quirky actress Elsa Lanchester, known for her iconic role as the monster's bride in the classic movie, 1935's ***The Bride of Frankenstein,*** *also appears in the Christmas movies* ***Come to the Stable*** *from 1949 as the religious painter, and* ***The Bishop's Wife*** *from 1947 as the family maid.*

Actor Michael Rooker who played serial killer Henry Lee Lucas in the 1986 film *Henry: Portrait of a Serial Killer* appears in a Christmas episode of the humorous spy show, *Chuck.* In 2008's "Chuck Versus the Santa Claus," lead character Chuck finds himself and the other employees at the electronics store being held hostage by a crazed gunman. Unfortunately, the hostage negotiator, played by Rooker, sent in to the store to help end the crisis is actually in cahoots with the gunman to ambush Chuck. This episode really makes one rethink last minute shopping!

Actor, Robert Englund, well-known for playing the

finger-blade wielding villain, Freddy Krueger in *The Nightmare on Elm Street* franchises, also appears in the 1980's TV series about alien invaders called *V: The Series*. In the 1984 holiday episode, "Reflection in Terror," the friendly alien, Willie, played by Englund fumbles the lyrics to "Deck the Halls" in the Club Creole. Later, Willie is seen in a Santa suit, eager to give out Christmas "pheasants."

And, actress Fellisa Rose, known for her role as the painfully shy, teen with a secret, Angela Barker from the 1983 summer camp slasher, *Sleepaway Camp*, is set to appear in the upcoming 2009 Christmas slash-fest, *Silent Night, Zombie Night*, a promising title if ever there was one.

Kids' Christmas: Not a Creature Was Stirring

Before the kids head off to bed, perhaps they too would like to enjoy an age-appropriate spooky story at Christmas. One possibility may be to watch the familiar gang from the Mystery Machine, in 2002's *A Scooby Doo Christmas*. In this modern update of the vintage series, Freddie and the gang stay overnight in a city that doesn't celebrate Christmas because its residents fear the Headless Snowman, a local monster that destroys people's chimneys. Is the culprit the hotel owner, eager to make money from people who are too scared to stay in their own homes? To add to the mystery, a local legend says there's stolen money to be found—who knows the most about it? This episode may be from the newer series, but it's far better than any of the Scrappy Doo episodes!

Another option for children may be 1979's animated TV special, *Casper's First Christmas*, featuring the friendliest little ghost. Living in a condemned house, Casper and fellow ghost Hairy Scary know this may be the last Christmas they spend there before it is torn down. Casper wants to celebrate Christmas, but Hairy doesn't believe in it. Meanwhile, Yogi Bear, Boo Boo, Quick Draw McGraw, Huckleberry Hound, Snagglepuss, Augie Doggie and Doggie Daddy take shelter on Christmas Eve in the condemned house after getting lost, while driving in their car. They begin to clean up and make the house cozy for their Christmas party, and true to character Casper is eager to make new friends. As usual, Hairy just wants to scare Casper's new friends away from the house and ruin their Christmas. In keeping with the spirit of the season, Hairy discovers Casper's generous letter to Santa asking for nothing but the deed to the house in Hairy's name. He is inspired to return Casper's friendship and invites Yogi's gang back in to celebrate Christmas again. This later Hanna-Barbera produced cartoon of the *Casper* franchise may not be the vintage *Casper* some of grew up watching, but it will still please and thrill young children.

Another possibility for the children might be the family-friendly series about a good witch married to a mortal. *Bewitched* has two Christmas episode where Samantha, played by Elizabeth Montgomery, actually appears in her black witch's outfit and pointy hat. In 1966's "A Vision of Sugar Plums," Sam dons her witchy finest to convince a little boy, who doesn't have much of a fantasy life, that Santa Claus and witches do exist. And, in 1967's "Humbug Not to Be Spoken Here," Sam wants to inspire the Christmas spirit in a client of Darren's who insists that he work on Christmas day. Once again, she costumes herself in her black garb in order to coax the client to ride her broomstick with her to the North Pole to meet the real Santa Claus as she teaches this scrooge a lesson he won't forget.

MYOM: NOT TOO COOL FOR YULE

While you're chillin' through the month of December, consider arranging your leisure time with the hippest and coolest in our popular culture. These iconic actors and artists are usually better known for other roles than these, but that makes these holiday films and TV episodes a rare treat, as well as an opportunity to spend your vacation time with the in-crowd.

Tough guy, Humphrey Bogart epitomizes Old School cool in a great Christmas movie as a Devil's Island escaped prisoner in 1955's *We're No Angels*. Director, Michael Curtiz, is also well-known for directing 1954's classic holiday film, *White Christmas,* as well as Bogie in 1942's *Casablanca. We're No Angels* was a rare comedic role for Bogart. Even more surprising, along with actors Aldo Ray and Peter Ustinov, Bogart sings a touching Christmas song about three angels to the family the three convicts stay with during their holiday dinner.

If you're not already familiar, discover Hollywood's Bad Boy, Robert Mitchum who appears in several notable holiday films. Mitchum plays the network boss, Preston Rhinelander, who is concerned with maximizing ad revenues from pet food sellers in 1988's *Scrooged*. It is Preston who ridiculously suggests that Frank Cross (Bill Murray's character) create more "pet appeal" in his TV productions to get cats and dogs watching TV. Mitchum also appears as the lead in the 1949 romance film *Holiday Affair,* as Steve Mason.

Bombshell legend, Marilyn Monroe, even briefly appeared in a Christmas movie. In the 1952 black-and-white film, *O. Henry's Full House,* five of the great American writer's short stories are adapted for the screen. The first vignette, based on the Christmas story "The Cop and the Anthem," is where viewers can spot Marilyn in an early role.

With his typical air of sophistication, actor Cary Grant stars in the 1947 Christmas movie *The Bishop's Wife* as Dudley, the debonair angel that comes to help Henry, the bishop, played by David Niven. Overworked Henry realizes fundraising for a new cathedral isn't as important as his marriage when he sees how happy his wife Julia, played by Loretta Young, is with the attention of the suave Dudley.

Sinatra's Rat Pack friends and fellow Vegas performers are unfailingly cool. Of course, Frank himself has a fantastic Christmas episode from his 1957 TV series, also referred to as *Happy Holidays With Bing and Frank* (see the Variety Chapter, pages 60-61). Sammy Davis Jr. appears in the 1990 holiday made-for-TV movie, *The Kid Who Loved Christmas*, his last film appearance before his death later that year. "The Greatest Living Entertainer" plays a jazz musician and friend to Tony, who is trying to adopt a young orphan boy at Christmas.

There were several Christmas specials produced for the successful *The Dean Martin Show*, variety TV series. True cult fans should dig up a copy of Dino's 1967 Christmas show, rumored to include the following guest stars: his good pal, Frank Sinatra; the Sinatra family, including Frank Jr., Tina and Nancy; as well as Martin's children and wife. While I haven't been able to find a copy for preview, hopefully this TV classic will be made available for purchase soon. True Rat Pack fans can't miss sitting through the two hour, 1964 film *Robin and the 7 Hoods* just to see the final scene in which Frank, Dino and Sammy appear in Santa suits, as broke but happy-go-lucky gangsters ringing their bells and panhandling on the streets of 1920s Chicago.

The next generation of Hollywood's coolest includes Paul Newman. He appeared, later in life, in the 1994 film that climaxes on New Year's Eve, *The Hudsucker Proxy*. Newman plays corporate bigwig, Sidney J. Mussburger.

Even the rugged, Steve McQueen can be seen in a 1958 Christmas episode of the western TV series *Wanted Dead or Alive*, entitled "Eight Cent Reward." McQueen plays the macho bounty hunter, Josh Randall, hired by a little boy on Christmas Eve for eight cents to find Santa Claus. This little boy, Laddie, played by child actor Jay North, desperately wants something from Santa but won't tell anyone else. Randall doesn't have the heart to turn down Laddie, so he arranges for the only man willing to dress as Santa, a local barfly, to talk to Laddie to get him to confess his secret Christmas wish. On Christmas Eve, it begins to snow heavily, and a passing stranger is forced to take shelter at Laddie's home. Meanwhile, the barfly is unable to convince Laddie he is Santa, and Randall is perplexed and disappointed. However, on Christmas morning, the boy finds his Christmas wish has come true while the stranger has mysteriously disappeared! This is an amazing episode—it's great TV to see tough guy, Steve McQueen working intently to make the little boy happy. The final scenes take an odd turn when it is revealed that what Laddie wanted so desperately was a rifle for his father—to kill the wolves preying on his father's sheep on their family ranch. The 1950s were a different era, weren't they?

People often forget that it was actress Natalie Wood who played the young, Susan Walker in the classic version of the film *Miracle on 34th Street* from 1947. The actress who immortalized her cool status by portraying the love interest, Judy, to James Dean's Jim in *Rebel Without a Cause*, had also been a child actress. Tears flow every time I see the film's final scene when Susan Walker recognizes her dream home, runs from the car, and finds Kris' cane propped up in the corner. I'm a sucker for a good split-level with an attached garage.

If beatnik, Greenwich Village subculture is your idea of cool, check out the short-lived TV series about the jazz musician turned private detective called *Johnny Staccato*, starring John Cassavetes. In the 1959 episode "The Unwise Men," Johnny takes a break from his jazz gig to help out a former musician friend who's moonlighting as a department store Santa and being blackmailed into assisting with the robbery of the store.

Also, Beat writer William Burroughs' holiday story of sacrifice was made into a stop motion, animated Christmas TV special called *The Junky's Christmas* in 1993. Taken from his book *Interzone*, the impressive stop motion story is also narrated by the aged writer, Burroughs himself. In this touching story, one junky is so moved by the pain of a fellow man in need of a fix that he sacrifices his own Christmas day portion in the spirit of the season.

In 1974, the low budget horror film, *Silent Night, Bloody Night* was unleashed at the theaters. This is your typical, unremarkable Christmas horror movie about incest, ax-wielding serial killers and escaped mental patients. What is remarkable about this film is that it features cult film actress, Mary Woronov. And, Woronov, Ondine, Candy Darling and several of the film's actors were notable Andy Warhol associates during the 1960s and regulars at the Factory, Warhol's creative epicenter.

If 1970s blaxploitation films are your version of cool, you must watch the parody holiday made-for-TV film, *The Hebrew Hammer* starring Adam Goldberg. This 2003 film spoofs the ultra-cool Shaft character from the popular 1970's hit movie franchise by creating a modern Jewish character named Mordechai Jefferson Carver, played by Goldberg, who is responsible for cleaning up the streets and saving Hanukkah. His arch nemesis is played by Andy Dick, so, yeah, hilarity ensues.

More 1970s subculture hipness includes the Japanese-made anime series *Lupin the 3rd* with the holiday episodes "The Sleight Before Christmas" and "Christmas At Tiffanys." In this highly stylized anime, an elite group of thieves work with the confident and snarky, international master thief, Lupin, who is always just out of reach of the law—personified by the daft, Inspector Zenigata. In the first holiday episode, Lupin sets his sights on the last bottle of Napoleon's bordeaux wine, even though it's being given to the President of the United States as a Christmas gift. Of course, there are several clever twists and turns as Lupin and his gang of tricksters deceive Zenigata. The highlight here is the look and feel of this vintage, ultra-cool Japanese animation and its suave title character. In the second holiday episode, "Christmas At Tiffanys," the Master Thief is at it again. This time he's asked to rob the world famous jewelry store, Tiffany's and Company, to see if he can break their impervious security system. It seems the owner, Maggie Tiffany, also works as a news anchor and is looking to broadcast the robbery on Christmas Eve, hoping to sweep the ratings. Lupin initially turns the challenge down but is forced to reconsider when Fujiko gets herself into debt after extravagantly shopping all over New York City.

If these examples of cool elude you, perhaps Milwaukee's motorcycle-riding hood from the '50s, Arthur "Fonzie" Fonzarelli, from *Happy Days* is more your style. Watch the four holiday episodes that feature story lines with Fonzie, including 1974's "Guess Who's Coming to Christmas," 1978's "Christmas Time," 1980's "White Christmas" and 1982's "All I Want for Christmas." Actor Henry Winkler has also appeared in several notable Christmas made-for-TV movies as well, the best of which are 1979's *An American Christmas Carol,* a Depression-era Scrooge story that takes place in New Hampshire rather than Victorian England, and 1994's *One Christmas,* based on the autobiographical short story written by American novelist, Truman Capote.

Christmas Stars and Men from Mars

Ever since the night in ancient Bethlehem when "that blessed star" illuminated the night sky, we've turned our gaze upwards at Christmas, searching for a connection to the heavens. We've come to expect angelic visitors from above delivering a message. As we look for meaning in the Christmas celebration, we expect to see wise visitors bearing gifts on a long journey from afar. The metaphorical stories of science fiction space travel and aliens seem to emanate organically from the original Nativity story. A continual reminder of our fascination with the heavens is that many of us ritually place a star atop our carefully decorated Christmas trees.

Following Yonder Star Wars

The place to start with sci-fi holiday material has to be the ever elusive, 1978 television spectacle, *The Star Wars Holiday Special.* It features much of the cast from the original film, including Mark Hamill, Carrie Fisher and Harrison Ford, as well as Chewbacca, Darth Vader, the Stormtroopers, C3-PO and R2-D2. Airing only once, this special became the stuff of legend: creator George Lucas ignores its existence; fans debate the rumors that it was the worst thing to ever air on TV, let alone the fact that it was a disappointment for *Star Wars* disciples. For years, bootleg VHS copies floated around college dorms. Then, it was sold illegally on Internet auction sites. Recently, it has become more accessible because of its instant availability over the Internet. But this has only served to prove to a wider, more curious audience with expectant high hopes just how incredibly awful it truly is.

Within the mythos of this galaxy far, far, away, they do not celebrate our Christmas but their own holiday called Life Day. When the story starts, Han Solo and Chewbacca are delayed from returning for the Life Day celebrations on the Wookie planet, Kashyyyk, because they are forced to battle Imperial ships along their route. Meanwhile, Chewie's family grows more worried with each passing hour of his absence, distracting themselves with mindless activities. His son, Lumpy, watches various entertainments on a hologram display. His wife, Malla, continues to prepare the holiday meal and watches a cooking demonstration on a video screen while Chewie's aged father, Itchy, concerns himself with more "adult" pursuits—indulging his fantasies with a virtual reality contraption, they call "a Mind Evaporator." Luke Skywalker checks in by way of a video screen as does Princess Leia to greet the Wookie family on the holiday, adding to growing tensions that Chewie and Han haven't yet arrived. Eventually, Darth Vader sends orders to catch the rebels by setting up a blockade around Kashyyyk, making it even more challenging for Chewbacca and Han Solo to return on Life Day. The Imperial guard turn up at the Wookie home and ransack the place looking for confirmation of their rebel sympathies, but Lumpy keeps himself busy watching an animated segment about his father and his friends on an adventure. When Chewbacca does finally return home, the family gathers to celebrate Life Day, where they each raise an orb to transport themselves to some enigmatic, celestial plane, reuniting with Luke, Han Solo, C3-PO, R2-D2 and Princess Leia, who sings a song about the holiday's meaning.

In the tradition of television holiday spectacles, there are musical numbers and special guest stars, including: Art Carney, who plays the pro-rebellion trading post owner and visitor to the Wookie home; comedic actor Harvey Korman appearing in several roles, including the cooking instructor, transmitter assembly teacher and a fawning customer in the cantina. Singer/actress Diahann Carroll appears as the sexy, fantasy singer in Itchy's Mind Evaporator; 1970s rock band Jefferson Starship (featuring Marty Balin) performs on a hologram display; and, singer/ actress Beatrice Arthur appears as the bartender at Mos

***Photo**: Harvey Korman and Bea Arthur in **The Star Wars Holiday Special** (1978).*

CBS/Photofest

Eisley's cantina and performs a boozy song.

There are a few good things about this special. Most of the original cast does appear in this television story. Mos Eisley's cantina scene gives us another look at the various alien life forms that gather there, and Princess Leia's Life Day song contains strains from several songs of John Williams' original music of the film. More importantly, this TV special is the first introduction of the bounty hunter, Boba Fett, a character who goes on to appear in the later films and captures the imagination of many *Star Wars* fans. However, there is far more that is disappointing about this TV special than what is good.

One major problem is that the story is too simple. It's obviously meant for children, but at two hours long, it's taxing for most attention spans. Much of the narrative is concerned with waiting. The main characters, Malla, Itchy and Lumpy sit around, trying to distract themselves with various entertainments while waiting for their loved one, Chewie to arrive. Viewers grow bored with waiting as well. The tension generated from the waiting is extended by the long segments of entertainment by the special guest stars while viewers only want to get through these pieces to see the action of their favorite *Star Wars* characters.

Making things worse, the guest stars aren't the sort to be relevant to children—but this doesn't mean it's more enjoyable to adult viewers either. The tone is usually wrong as well. Harvey Korman in drag, playing the cooking instructor with multiple arms, or as the inane robotic teacher providing assembly instructions for Lumpy's transmitter, can't help but fail. Could children ever find Bea Arthur's song endurable? And, synthesizer-heavy, Grace Slick-absent, Jefferson Starship? Only in a galaxy far, far, away.

It's difficult to describe the errors, because they are numerous. However, the clearest problem is that the special doesn't provide viewers with enough excitement and new story to add to the original fascination with the *Star Wars* movie. Annoyance with George Lucas creations is something more familiar to contemporary audiences (I'm referring specifically to Jar Jar Binks), but in 1978 it was quite a disappointing shock. Somehow, I think, having recognizable celebrities seen interacting within the *Star Wars* milieu also reduces the fantastic, otherworldly nature of the story—constantly reminding viewers that they are watching a TV holiday special like so many others, rather than the more precious world of our then-favorite fantasy heroes.

If you crave Christmas that actually feels like more of the *Star Wars* universe, check out the 1997 animated TV special, *Santa Vs. Snowman*. Here, Santa Claus recalls a previous holiday when a lonely snowman became jealous of Santa's worldwide adulation, deciding to wage war against Santa's Village for control of Christmas. The snowman creates an ice army of snow minions that attack the North Pole in battle scenes that evoke *Star Wars Episode V: The Empire Strikes Back*. The snowman's forces attacking the elf battalions resemble the fight against the Imperial forces on the ice planet Hoth in the 1980 film. This project, created by master storyteller, Steve Oedekerk, has since been reworked into a 3-D experience for IMAX theaters and has been shown around the world.

Classic Sci-fi Christmases

If the *Star Wars Holiday Special* disappoints the sci-fi nerd in you, there are other classics of the genre telling a Christmas story that may capture your interest. An episode of the 1985 revival of *The Twilight Zone* features a story based on an interpretation of the Hugo award-winning, Arthur C. Clarke short story "The Star." In the future, a team of scientists exploring space lands upon a planet's surface and discovers a cache of artifacts put there by a previous human civilization that has since died out due to their sun going supernova. A scientist/priest tries to reconcile the justification of such a tremendous loss of human life with God's plan for the universe. His calculations show him that this planet's sun's supernova was surely the bright star that shown in the sky on Earth that fateful Christmas in Bethlehem. The captain of the crew reminds the priest that what appears to him as the capriciousness of God was actually part of the hopeful cycle of life. While some died because of the supernova, others experienced a life-changing, new light on planet Earth which impacted the whole of human culture.

There is some controversy amongst sci-fi fans about this episode's story since it is an interpretation of the classic Clarke story. The original story ends without the captain's more optimistic message that's been added to the TV episode. Though the episode adheres to the strict TV tradition of providing Christmas stories with happy endings, this seems more like an extension of the original Clarke story, and less like an insincere rewrite. But you can judge for yourself.

More recently, Terry Pratchett, the prolific British sci-fi/fantasy author, saw his book, *Hogfather* adapted for a 2006 made-for-TV movie. This two-part, mini-series Christmas story takes place in Pratchett's well-known mythic Disc World. The complex story of the Hogfather (a parallel to Father Christmas or Santa Claus) begins with the loss of the annual gift bringer, a role that has to be taken up by another on Hogswatch Eve. Death (voiced by Ian Richardson) puts down his sickle and black robe to don the red suit of Hogfather and ride the hog-pulled sleigh through the night to deliver the toys, accompanied by his assistant, Albert (played by actor, David Jason). Death's granddaughter Susan uncovers a complex magical conspiracy, lead by Mr. Teatime, to take control over people's beliefs and fantasies. The conspiracy jeopardizes not only the future of Hogfather, the Tooth Fairy and the other small fictions we choose to value but the big fictions of the human world as well, such as Justice and Truth. The complicated story is a struggle to comprehend at times, but the reward is great if you can hold out through the four hour length of the mini-series. Not only is the richness of the fantasy of the Discworld worth the effort, but the high production values, amazing cast, and the philosophical implications about the human need for fantasy and for Christmas are exciting. Don't miss the author himself, Terry Pratchett, playing the role of the Toymaker in the movie's final scene.

Christmas With the Doctor

The contemporary revival of the long-running British TV sci-fi institution, *Doctor Who,* has produced several recent big budget Christmas specials. In 2005's "The Christmas Invasion" the Doctor and his companion, Rose, arrive at her home in London for Christmas. The Doctor is weak from the Time Lord regeneration process. As the Doctor sleeps in a coma, the British Prime Minister faces an alien invasion from the Sycorax—a race of beings that have hypnotized one third of the human population and are blackmailing the Minister into agreeing to a surrender of the whole of Earth.

2006's "Runaway Bride," sees a bride mysteriously transported into the TARDIS. The Doctor and the bride, Donna, discover that from an eight-pointed star in the Christmas night sky, the Empress of the Racnoss schemes to free the other members of the Racnoss race. Apparently, they were buried at the center of the Earth at its formation and Donna is their key to freedom. Fans of the show will know that the character of Donna, played by comedian Catherine Tate, will return two seasons later as the Doctor's companion. This Christmas special's story is revisited in the episode "Turn Left" in 2008.

In 2007's "Voyage of the Damned," the Doctor stows away on a luxury cruise ship orbiting Earth. The alien ship is there to partake of the Earth custom of Christmas but the vessel is sabotaged and set on a collision course with the planet while all the survivors are being eliminated by the ship's Christmas-themed information robots called Heavenly Hosts. Though the luxury spaceship is named the Titanic, this story evokes the 1972 disaster film, *The Poseidon Adventure* which also takes place aboard a sinking cruise ship at holiday time.

In 2008's "The New Doctor," the Doctor returns to Victorian London on Christmas Eve, 1851, where he bumps into another man claiming to be the Doctor. But there is even more trouble this Christmas in London: the Cybermen have kidnapped a workforce of children to generate electricity to power a skyscraper-sized CyberKing. This is in addition to their usual cyber-nasty plan: to transform millions of humans into more deadly robotic cybermen. The story uses the familiar Dickensian theme of impoverished, orphan children being exploited to strike its emotional tone of desperation as the two Doctors rush to stop the villains.

Dedicated fans of the series may also remember the 2005 episode, "The Unquiet Dead." Though it didn't originally air at Christmas time, it does take place on Christmas Eve and involves the Doctor stopping in London in 1869 and visiting the popular author, Charles Dickens, who is busy with his public readings of *A Christmas Carol*. The Doctor discovers a funeral parlor with a problem: the corpses keep coming back to life! The Time Lord works with the Londoners to aid the gaseous aliens requiring corporeal bodies to survive. These aliens reanimating corpses make it seem as if Dickens' ghosts have come to life.

Doctor Who completists—you know who you are—may know that a Christmas message spoken by the Doctor, played by William Hartnell in 1965's "The Feast of Steven" from the serial "The Daleks' Master Plan" has long gone missing and is presumed erased. However, amateur audio of the original broadcast can still be acquired.

An air of excitement surrounds this 2008 Christmas special as it reunites actors David Morrissey and David Tennant. These two worked together before as arch-nemeses in the 2004 groundbreaking TV program, ***Blackpool****, a dynamic murder mystery series that was also a musical.*

Additionally, another Christmas installment can be found in the only episode of the failed spin-off *K-9 and Company* entitled, "A Girl's Best Friend," originally broadcast in 1981. Here, the popular companion Sarah Jane Smith becomes acquainted with the robot/computer dog, K-9. Together, they confront a rural community's black magic ritual of human sacrifice at the Winter Solstice. Nothing quite says Merry Christmas like pentagrams, goats and hooded black robes.

The contemporary *Doctor Who* spin-off series, *Torchwood* has a holiday installment in the first season's "Out of Time." Captain Jack and his staff welcome two passengers and the pilot of a plane that journey through a time rift, taking off at Christmas in 1953 but landing in 2006. The accidental time travelers find it difficult to adjust to modern mores and futures without their loved ones.

Projections of Christmases Future From the Past

The groundbreaking Apollo 8 moon orbit mission broadcast the three NASA astronauts offering their seasons greetings on Christmas Eve 1968, with each taking his turn reading from the book of Genesis' creation story. This historical Christmas Eve broadcast won television's highest award, an Emmy. It also historically connected TV with space travel and the yuletide. But television hadn't waited for this momentous occasion to begin airing sci-fi holiday episodes. These pre-Apollo 8 installments were created as futuristic visions of Christmases yet to come. Can any of us imagine what Christmas will be like in the year 2000?

In 1951, the American children's program, *Space Patrol,* produced a Christmas episode which takes place in the futuristic 30th century. Commander Buzz Corey secretly arranges to have Cadet Happy's parents flown in from planet Earth to surprise Hap for Christmas. Unfortunately, Hap feels lonely and isolated from the others, having been sent away on a useless errand so the others can arrange the Christmas party. When it's time to start the party, they can't find Hap to show him their surprise.

In 1953, the comedy series, *The Paul Winchell Show* also created a Christmas episode where ventriloquist Paul imagines Christmases past, present and future with his wooden dummy, Jerry Mahoney. In a projection of Christmas in the year 2000, Paul imagines flying to the popular tourist resort, the Moon. Dressed in amazing retro silver flight uniforms, Paul and Jerry are saddened to discover that Moon people don't celebrate Christmas. Check out Jerry's futuristic astro-helmet and Paul's ray gun.

In 1963, a Christmas episode of the Japanese anime series *Astro Boy* entitled, "The Wonderful Christmas

Present" was produced. This classic cartoon features the powerful android, Astro Boy, going to Snow Cone Mountain for a Christmas vacation accompanied by Astro Girl. There, they meet Miyo, an orphan who is being well taken care of by a technologically advanced home filled with robots. The robots were invented by Miyo's father before he died, and criminals want to steal the plans, forcing Astro Boy to protect the home. This story also takes place in the year 2000 and the title refers to the comforting, healthful, nurturing environment that the mechanized home provides. Better living through appliances.

But hands down, the far most interesting projection of Christmases future has come more recently in the vision created by the animated series, *Futurama* in the 1999 episode, "Xmas Story." In the year 3000, Christmas is much different than it once was: Xmas substitutes palm for pine trees and Santa is an evil robot killing machine that comes to punish everyone—his naughty/nice evaluator is gauged too high. Christmas Eve is spent by most people hiding from the dangerous Santa robot. Fry leaves safety to buy Leela a Christmas present but he ends up running for his life, chased by the evil robot Santa.

In the follow-up 2000 episode entitled "A Tale of Two Santas," the crew flies to the North Pole of Neptune to deliver letters to Santa, which beg him not to visit and destroy the Earth. While there, they incapacitate the evil Santa allowing Bender to take up the role of the good, generous toy-delivering Santa role—however, no one is expecting a good Santa and he's captured and sentenced to be executed for Santa's previous crimes and destruction. Look for the scene in which Bender meets the other holiday icon on his annual rounds, the Kwanzaa-bot, voiced by rapper, Coolio.

*Photo: Bender, Leela and Fry meet the evil Robot Santa in **Futurama's** "Xmas Story" (1999).*

Fox Broadcasting/ Photofest

Hidden Gems: Join the Triumph of the Skies

Dubbed into English with Cyrillic credits, the 1959 public domain cartoon from Cold War Russia, commonly called *Christmas Visit,* is well worth finding. A little boy named Kolya lives in Moscow and misses his father at Christmas time. His father works as a weatherman in Antarctica. Kolya wishes he could bring his father a Christmas tree and decides to make the journey to the South Pole to bring his father a tree. At the start of his quest, Kolya receives help from Santa Claus, who loans him his "star studded jet plane" to serve as his transportation to the farthest corner of the planet. The little boy and his Christmas tree fly across the night sky in the rocket ship, getting caught in a sandstorm in Africa where he crash lands. Though Kolya has a deadline to return Santa's rocket, the boy continues his journey to deliver the tree, making friends with animals that assist his travels such as a lion, monkeys, a whale and penguins. Kolya awakens at home, discovering his journey was just a dream—only to learn that his father did in fact receive a Christmas tree delivered by plane. What makes this cartoon unique is the jet plane Santa uses for transportation is a fantastic '50s-era rocket ship! This is also known under the title, *Santa Claus Visits Antarctica*.

There's also the kitschy 1964 feature length film *Santa Claus Conquers the Martians*, directed by Nicholas Webster. In this bizarre cult classic, Martian children watch Santa Claus on Earth television and want to meet this incredible man. So their Martian parents journey to Earth to kidnap him—however they can't tell which man dressed in red is the real Santa! They grab young Americans Billy and Betsy to accompany them to the North Pole to identify the correct Santa. Once on board their space craft and traveling to Mars however, Santa easily charms all the Martians but one: the wicked, Voldar. Santa convinces the Martians that there is joy in making and giving toys to children but Voldar wants to permanently get rid of Santa. The most entertaining way to watch this movie is to find it on *Mystery Science Theater 3000*, the TV series that adds wicked and culturally savvy commentary over cult classics. The *MST 3k* treatment is fun to watch with its comment on this film's cheesy dialogue, low-budget space equipment and kooky Martian costumes. Also, the *MST 3k* characters add more to the Christmas celebration during the breaks from the movie segments.

And, in 2008 Wayne Coyne of the alternative rock band The Flaming Lips finally released his bizarre version of a

Christmas *2001: A Space Odyssey.* In the movie, *Christmas on Mars,* it's Christmas Eve on a doomed Mars space station and the crew is succumbing to madness due to a lack of adequate oxygen production and the realization of their own human "cosmic reality" or insignificance in the universe. Major Syrtis, played by band member, Steven Drozd, becomes alarmed when Ed 15, the man he had enlisted to be the crew's Santa Claus, commits suicide. A green alien, played by band front man, Wayne Coyne, arrives from out of the darkness, and is recruited to fill in as Santa for the Christmas party. Hope returns to the space station when a healthy baby is born on board, putting an end to the crews' fears and nightmares. The film contains sequences in both black-and-white and color, embracing a 1960s vintage look to the space station and vision of the future. It's loaded with delightful, homemade special effects and the set design gives it a distinctly retro, sci-fi atmosphere. It's also easy to see Coyne's love for influential filmmakers, such as Stanley Kubrick and David Lynch, in this quirky, stylized Christmas film.

The vintage, classic 1955 futuristic movie, ***Conquest of Space*** *is not really a holiday film, however it does contain a Christmas scene. The elite group of astronauts on Mars are stuck waiting for an optimal time to leave the red planet. As their water reservoir levels diminish, they note the passage of time by remarking that the calendar says its Christmas. Marvelously, it snows on Mars, providing the astronauts their much needed water supply to survive until they can return to their home space station, orbiting Earth. Another freakin' Christmas miracle.*

Comedic Alien Visitors

It is a part of the mythos of the holiday to expect visitors from afar and television has brought us many comedies about the most distant of visitors, space aliens in fact, living right here on Earth amongst us. A typical holiday story line for those from outer space focuses on a misunderstanding of the complexity of the traditions of the season. For example, 1978's *Mork & Mindy* episode, "Mork's First Christmas" sees the One from Ork following Mindy's description of holiday spirit by inviting the much-loathed, shallow and egotistical Susan, played by Morgan Fairchild, to their home for Christmas. Mork also prepares homemade gifts for the McConnell family, and though his gifts go under-appreciated, he is able to give better gifts once he understands the adage "it's the thought that counts." His alien abilities allow him to affect them each with a treasured thought from their pasts.

Also in 1986's "Oh Tannerbaum" from the hit show, *Alf,* the title alien life form begins his first Christmas by unknowingly chopping the Tanner family Christmas tree into firewood. He endears himself to the Tanners in other ways that Christmas—including buying them each a gift. However, he does all his shopping from one source: a hardware catalog.

3rd Rock from the Sun's 1996 hilarious episode "Jolly Old St. Dick" sees the Solomon family aliens celebrating their first Christmas with continual holiday missteps. Dick is embittered by the hypocrisy between Christmas spirit and how people really act. Harry finds a job working as Santa's assistant and Sally works wrapping presents at the mall. Tommy is worried about buying his girlfriend, August, the perfect gift. Harry is frightened by the possible true identity of Santa and Sally begins substituting more appropriate gifts for the ones the customers actually purchased. Dick has his usual freak-out, throwing holiday decorations off the roof at carolers. One thing they get right is that Harry brings home a Christmas tree just like Charlie Brown's little tree.

The British comedy series starring comedian/actor Ardal O'Hanlon called *My Hero,* serializes the adventures of George Sunday, who comes to Earth offering his alien abilities to aid as the superhero Thermo Man. In 2000's "Christmas" episode, George is just as confused about Christmas traditions as he is of all Earth customs. When his friends don't seem to be enjoying Christmas, Thermo

Man acts as Father Christmas, surprising them with gifts under their trees on Christmas morning. However, his sweet surprise is misunderstood and everyone fears that their homes were broken into. Later, George brings the real Santa to them, who offers them any one gift of their choosing. In disbelief, no one takes Santa's offer very seriously, each requesting junk from the man who can make their dreams come true.

Always a holiday favorite is the 2002 holiday chapter "The Most Horrible Christmas Ever" of the animated series *Invader Zim*. Ever searching for another grandiose world-conquest strategy, the alien disguised as a schoolboy creates a technologically advanced Santa Claus suit, so he can be worshipped at Christmas time and in turn, enslave the entire human population of Earth. However, the suit also contains all the "good will" of the season downloaded into its computer which ultimately prevents Zim's evil takeover.

Kids' Christmas: The Stars Are Brightly Shining

George and the Christmas Star is a Canadian-made, animated classic from 1985. It's well worth the search for this difficult to find but charming story. George has a paper star for the top of his Christmas tree but decides he wants something better. So he builds a rocket ship to go into space to get the one he spots in his telescope. In space, he meets Ralph, an alien robot who joins George on his search for the perfect star. Along the way, they are attacked by space pirates and taken hostage aboard their ship where they meet Barbara, another hostage. Space police rangers come and free the three new friends, but they run into more trouble with outlaw space bikers, called the Bells

Angels. They escape and find George's star, putting it in a box. The friends don't have enough fuel to get home until Santa flies by, and agrees to help them. Back at home, George, Ralph and Barbara put the star on top of his tree but it floats back up into space! This charming animated special also includes songs written and performed by musical legend Paul Anka.

Another rare but adorable classic children's special is 1977's *A Cosmic Christmas*, an animated tale with a distinctive, stylized character design. Here, Peter and his pet goose Lucy wander the busy downtown streets at Christmas time. While looking at a crèche in a store's window display, Peter sees the reflection of a moving light in the sky, and believes he's seen a U.F.O. Later, walking in the woods, Peter meets three aliens from the spaceship who have come to investigate the 2000-year-old Star of Bethlehem. Peter tries to explain the meaning of Christmas to the visitors but struggles to show them examples in the city of the love, peace, generosity and good will as he described them. That is, until Peter falls through the ice, pursuing the hungry teen who stole his pet goose. The city folk gather to pull Peter out of the frozen pond and with the understanding of the visiting spacemen, come to see that Christmas is about people coming together to help one another. As the visitors from space fly away, they leave behind a beautiful night display of an angel in the sky.

And in 1991, a unique children's animated special, *Aliens First Christmas*, gave a new perspective to holiday nostalgia. Earthlings Fran and Roger Peoples are living with their son Benny on the planet Zolonia in the year 2027. While still trying to adapt to their new surroundings, they experience an even rougher time at Christmas because their Earth celebration is completely foreign to those around them.

In ***The Star Wars Holiday Special****, the animated segment that Lumpy watches on his viewer—the same that introduces the bounty hunter character, Boba Fett—was produced by the Canadian animation studio, Nelvana, which has since grown into one of the largest animation producers in the world. They are also responsible for creating* ***A Cosmic Christmas****.*

The Peoples' next-door neighbors, Charlick and Mavo Zox, decide to try to help their new 'alien' friends recreate their holiday even if they don't understand it. It's funny to see how the Zolonians misinterpret our familiar traditions, e.g.: a Santa Clocks that ho-ho-hoes in the garden, stockings hanging over the fireplace are set on fire, and a decorated spine tree for a Hairy Christmas. But the Zoxs' generosity and love for their neighbors is the true spirit of the season after all and appreciated by the "aliens."

MYOM:
Where No Christmas Has Gone Before

Beyond the disappointment of *The Star Wars Holiday Special,* some sci-fi fans may feel cheated by the lack of a classic *Star Trek* holiday installment. But don't let that show's writers keep you from making your final frontier Christmas dreams come true. Below you'll find suggestions for generating your own *Star Trek* yuletide experience.

TV Legend William Shatner has appeared in a wide variety of holiday productions over the years. However, consider his recent appearance on the law series *Boston Legal,* specifically 2007's "Green Christmas" where Shatner's over-the-top character Denny Crane dons blinking reindeer antlers. Shatner also makes a grand appearance in the made-for-TV holiday movie *A Carol Christmas* alongside co-star Tori Spelling. In this contemporary retelling of the Dickens' classic, he plays Dr. Bob, a neurotic, self-help TV talk show host who becomes the Ghost of Christmas Present.

Leonard Nimoy can be heard as the voice of a Greek nobleman in the 1983 animated history of the Jewish people and Hanukkah entitled *Lights*. Here the "lights" cleverly represent more than just the flames burning in the temple of Jerusalem's oil lamps or modern menorah candles, but the Word of God and the rich legacy of the Jewish people. The animated story begins when God first gave the "lights" to mankind at Mt. Sinai and continues up to the Greek Empire's influence and suppression of Jewish faith and culture. Along with the voice talents of actors Judd Hirsch and Paul Michael Glaser, this inspirational TV special depicts the rich cultural heritage of Nimoy and Judaism.

Some TV fans may feel a loyalty to Captain Jean-Luc Picard from the first of the follow-up series, the very successful *Star Trek: The Next Generation* which began airing in 1987. Actor Patrick Stewart appeared in the well-received 1999 made-for-TV movie, *A Christmas Carol,* in the lead role as Ebenezer Scrooge. The 1994 feature length film, *Star Trek: Generations*—the seventh movie in the franchise—includes an interesting holiday scene. Though not a holiday-themed film, it contains a sequence with Picard in the temporal Nexus, experiencing a fantasy of a Christmas day spent with his own wife and children. He knows it to be so profoundly unreal that he withdraws from it, and seeks the help of Capt. Kirk (Shatner) to bring a stop to Soran's plan of destruction. Kirk and Picard, two great tastes that taste great together.

If your Christmas *Trek* appetite is whetted, consider watching a yuletide episode from an earlier series by *Star Trek*'s creator and executive producer, Gene Roddenberry. One such, is "The Hanging Cross" of the TV series *Have Gun, Will Travel.* In much the same tone and moralistic manner of the familiar space program, this 1957 Roddenberry-written western sees Paladin attempting to mediate a custody negotiation between the Pawnee indians and a rancher who's son was stolen and now raised by the tribesmen. While the rancher is committed to bloody revenge, Paladin calls for a nonviolent solution on Christmas Eve in the spirit of the season.

MYOM: SECOND CHANCE CHRISTMAS SPECIALS

Christmas TV specials have grown to achieve a cult status of their own: these emotional and sentimental favorites are only broadcast once a year. Many are never seen more than once because they are replaced by new specials. More contemporary specials will be released on DVD, but many of the older specials can only be viewed by the few who remember their titles, either online or when an old VHS copy can be found by someone with the compatible player. Far more were never even released for home viewing on VHS in the first place. Below are several older cult Christmas TV specials that are far from forgotten and certainly worth rediscovering.

If you grew up in Chicago or the Midwest, then you may remember the repeated airings, or your older family members constantly talking about the following three Christmas animated shorts: *Hardrock, Coco, and Joe: The Three Little Dwarfs, Suzy Snowflake* and *Frosty the Snowman*. The first short is based on the song "The Three Little Dwarfs" by Stuart Hamblen. It aired on Chicago's WGN alongside *Suzy Snowflake* and *Frosty the Snowman* since the early 1950s. *Hardrock, Coco and Joe* is a delightful, black-and-white, stop motion short that tells the story of Santa's three helper-elves, Hardrock, the driver, Coco, the map reader and the beloved Joe, riding in Santa's sleigh on Christmas Eve. Likewise, *Suzy Snowflake* is an animated, black-and-white short, based on the 1951 song "Suzy Snowflake" written by Sid Tepper and Roy Brodsky, about the wintertime fairy, who taps on your window pane, helps build snowmen and takes sleigh rides. And, *Frosty the Snowman* is another musical story that follows the lyrics of the popular song, in a black-and-white, animated short. This cartoon is quintessential 1950s, set to a swinging jazz arrangement of the song that has gone on to inspire many animated retellings.

Few who have seen it will ever forget the 1969 TV special story of the young Harlem kid, *J.T.* Originally produced for CBS'

Saturday morning *Children's Hour,* this emotional tale has also aired in primetime and has won the prestigious Peabody Award. A troubled little boy living in the ghetto finds his connection to the world through a sickly cat he cares for in an abandoned building. As Christmas approaches, J.T.'s transistor radio is stolen and he's chased by two bullies from the condemned building, only to witness his cat run over in the street by a car. A despondent J.T. is consoled by his visiting grandmother. Later at Christmas, the boy's life is transformed when the neighborhood grocer gives J.T. a kitten and a chance at a new start. This story can warm the coldest of hearts. It stars actor Kevin Hooks as the young lead. Hooks is recognizable from his later role as Morris Thorpe, on the TV series *The White Shadow* and he currently works as a director for dramatic TV series. J.T.'s mother is played by actress Ja'net DuBois who also appeared as the upstairs neighbor, Willona on the long running, 1970s sitcom, *Good Times.*

Another quality TV special from 1969 is *The Littlest Angel,* a Hallmark Hall of Fame production and musical adaptation of the popular book authored by Charles Tazewell. Here redheaded child actor, Johnny Whitaker plays the young angel, Michael, who doesn't like Heaven very much. The unhappy eight year-old angel doesn't know how to fly, he's much younger than the other angels and he's homesick. His guardian angel, Patience, played by Fred Gwynne, tries to help him get flying lessons and to fit in so he can enjoy paradise, but to no avail. Michael is eventually allowed a brief return to his earthly home, to retrieve his favorite box of things, which includes: a dog collar, several broken birds eggs, a couple of river stones, a feather and a butterfly. Once he's back in Heaven, all the other angels are busy preparing for the birth of God's son and planning their gifts. While the other angels have made precious gifts, befitting royalty, Michael has nothing to offer except his favorite box of treasures. Although he's embarrassed by its inadequacies, he humbly shares his most prized possessions.

However, God is pleased with Michael's generosity and turns the humble gift into the bright Star of Bethlehem.

If you can get over the fact that Michael is a homesick, little dead boy, who is unhappy with being sent to Heaven, then the story can be sweet. This version of the popular Christmas story was originally produced on videotape and so it lacks the image quality of a filmed production. However, the casting is superb and more than makes up for the low image quality and budget chroma-key special effects. Moreover, who would have known that actor Fred Gwynne, fondly remembered for his patriarchal role as Herman Munster on the 1960s TV series *The Munsters* would have a lovely singing voice? In addition to Whitaker and Gwynne, this production also includes beloved actor Tony Randall as the philosophical angel Democritus, music legend Cab Calloway as the angel Gabriel, actress Connie Stevens as the Flying Mistress and E.G. Marshall as God.

A series of children's animated specials with a religious leaning were created on behalf of a Lutheran ministries group in the early 1970s that follow two characters: the young boy, Benji and his sheep dog, Waldo. The first of these productions from 1970, is entitled, *Christmas Is*. Here, Benji has been cast in the Christmas pageant as the second shepherd once again, but he's not sure what his role means. As he rereads the biblical story, he and Waldo find themselves transported back in time, to Bethlehem. While he finds room at the inn serving food to the guests, he sees that other travelers are turned away. He hears the others talking about the coming Messiah, and he awakens in the middle of the night by the light of a bright star. Benji learns that the news of the Christ child's birth would not have been known without the shepherds. Aroused from sleep, Benji rushes to the pageant, eager to play his role in the Nativity story. Benji and Waldo have additional adventures in the Christmas special *The City That Forgot About Christmas*, the Easter special, *Easter Is* and the Fourth of July special, *Freedom Is*.

One made-for-TV movie that casts a long shadow is the 1972 tearjerker—as in, you will want to keep a full box of tissues handy—*The House Without a Christmas Tree*. This story takes place in Nebraska, 1946 and is based on the best selling children's book written by Gail Rock. The story focuses on ten year-old Addie Mills who has never had a Christmas tree and doesn't understand why her father won't allow her to have one this year. We see Addie's father, played by the late great character actor, Jason Robards, explaining to her grandmother that a Christmas tree reminds him of his wife who died when Addie was a baby. He's too bitter about the painful loss and doesn't want to feel happy at the holiday—even though Addie has no idea about the pain he feels and its connection to Christmas. It seems everyone else in school celebrates the holiday in a traditional way—why can't she? On the last day of school before Christmas vacation, Addie wins a contest and the prize is the classroom tree. However once at home, her father demands that she remove it, insisting that they should not accept charity when they aren't poor. Addie drags the tree to a classmate's home—a girl whose family is poor and doesn't have a tree. Seeing this, her father has a change of heart and brings home a tree for Addie. He gives her a star for the top—a special ornament her mother made before she died. As you can imagine, Robards is convincing as the gruff, grumpy, and emotionally withdrawn father. When he finally brings the star out from the attic and gives it to his daughter, you'll know why I warned you to have a full box of tissues at the ready.

Comedian Molly Shannon played the incredibly funny reoccurring character Mary Katherine Gallagher on ***Saturday Night Live****. In a 1996 Christmas sketch, Shannon's hand-sniffing klutzy Catholic school girl appeared alongside Whitney Houston, Penny Marshall and Rosie O' Donnell. She steals the stage in the school pageant's rehearsal to quote from the cult film* ***The House Without A Christmas Tree****.*

Another cult Christmas TV special that was also underwritten by the Lutherans is the 1979 live-action program, *The Stableboy's Christmas*. In this story, a little girl named Tammy, played by child actress Danielle Brisebois, wraps a new doll as a gift that she wishes she could keep for herself, but her mother scolds her for not showing the true generous spirit of Christmas. During a tantrum, Tammy throws herself under the family Christmas tree and the little stableboy in the wooden Nativity display comes to life. He works for the innkeeper in Bethlehem. Mary and her husband Joseph arrive in town looking for a room, and the stableboy lets them use the animal shelter behind the inn. That night he directs the shepherds and the three wise men to the newborn. The stableboy even gives the Christ child his very own lamb as a gift. Tammy eventually awakens from under the Christmas tree with a greater understanding of generosity at Christmas time.

What's fun about this fantasy story is that nearly every actor in this program is recognizable from 1970s television and earlier: the stableboy, played by child actor, Sparky Marcus also appeared in the TV version of *The Bad News Bears* as Ogilvie. Danielle Brisebois, who plays Tammy, is well-known for her role as Stephanie on the later episodes of *All in the Family*. The innkeeper is played by William Schallert who also appeared as Patty's father on *The Patty Duke Show*, among many other roles. The Roman soldier is played by Dave Madden—also known for his iconic role as Reuben Kincaid on *The Partridge Family*. Joseph is portrayed by actor Jerry Houser, who also appeared as Wally, Marcia's husband on *A Very Brady Christmas*; and there are many more recognizable character actors. For those that grew up watching TV in the 1970s or those that love playing the game "who's who," this Christmas special is a rare treat of celebrity spotting.

And, another gone-but-not-forgotten TV program is the often educational, children's series, *Young People's Specials*. Two installments from this series are holiday stories with the continuing character Charlie, played by a very young, Seth Green. 1984's episode, *Charlie's Christmas Secret* sees the title character feeling like the only kid at school without the Christmas spirit and fearing he may be getting too old for it. Over the holiday break, he asks everyone along his paper route about their feelings for Christmas and what makes them happy. When he finds that several of his friends and neighbors are also without joy during the holiday, Charlie finds that he can create the right spirit by making other people's holidays special. He invites those in need to his own family's Christmas dinner and spends his own gift money on presents for others. In a later episode entitled *Charlie's Christmas Project,* the dogcatcher takes in the stray dog Charlie has been feeding in a back alley. Although his parents won't let him have a dog, Charlie doesn't want Arfy to be put to sleep on Christmas Eve. He desperately tries to find a home for the dog amongst his neighbors, as well as the other animals at the pound, but it's hard work. His friend, Mr. Smith, a homeless man, tries to help Charlie but his efforts also fall short until Christmas Eve, when a miracle happens. Charlie's commitment persuades his friends to open their hearts. Both of these tender stories are sweet reminders of the power of a generous spirit at holiday time. It's great fun watching the hip, edgy actor and a creative force behind the funny series *Robot Chicken* in this early, poignant role.

From Our TV Family to Yours: Variety Christmas Extravaganzas

There is a grand tradition on television of creating flashy, musical spectacles at holiday time. Big budgets are allocated to adorn extravagant sets, out come the Victorian period costumes and there are always special celebrity guest stars. In the earlier days of TV when variety shows were ubiquitous, each one featured a special Christmas installment. Every year, singer Perry Como would travel to another festive spot on the globe for his yuletide show. Bing Crosby would introduce his beautiful young wife and their children before singing "White Christmas" again, and Andy Williams would embrace four-part harmony with his talented brothers, while showcasing the similarly talented but much younger and equally clean-cut, Osmond Brothers.

The Really Big Show: Historical Moments

Several of these TV events, representing the height of traditional variety shows, have grown into legendary significance within the history of the medium. One such is the 1963 Christmas episode of the short-lived *The Judy Garland Show,* starring singers, Jack Jones and Mel Tormé, as well as Garland's children, Joe, Lorna and Liza. The show opens with the camera looking through the windows of a home, focusing on the maternal Miss Garland singing the melancholy "Have Yourself a Merry Little Christmas" while affectionately grasping Joe and Lorna. Of course, this is the memorable song that she made popular in the 1944 movie, *Meet Me in St. Louis*. Judy invites the TV cameras into her home for this Christmas TV special, to share the holiday with her family as her good friends, Jack Jones and Mel Tormé informally drop by. Both young Joe and Lorna adorably sing off-key songs, and a 17 year-old, Liza Minnelli is here entertaining too—the best is her song and dance jazz number to "Steam Heat." Garland and her children sing and dance ever so casually, as if improvising, yet the choreography and the off-stage orchestration suggests otherwise. In fact, all the entertainment appears informal—as if a natural extension of the singer's lifestyle, yet it's so perfectly conceived and painstakingly arranged, it can't be that natural. Twice when a team of stylized Santa Clauses raucously bursts through Garland's front door to dance in the middle of her living room, the audience is once again reminded of how phony this improvised moment truly must be. Despite her professional demeanor, Judy really seems to be uncomfortable, at times appearing to be forcing the Christmas spirit.

Hollywood legend says that Garland's short-lived variety show had been plagued with problems. Some blame her drinking as well as backstage egos. Whether you're aware of the rumors or not, problems are palpable on the production of her Christmas Show. Garland herself is ill-at-ease during the taping. She seems distracted and fidgety, not really focused during the entire show. And later, tension can be felt when Garland sits at the piano to sing with Tormé, the song so synonymous with the holiday, that it's often overlooked that Tormé himself co-wrote it—"The Christmas Song." Harmonizing along side the "Velvet Fog," Judy accidentally flubs a line and Tormé reacts jovially, laughing and making the aside comment, "Close...." But there is clearly some friction when Judy purposefully alters the next line to add a lyric from her signature tune "Over the Rainbow" on top of his masterpiece. The first lyric change was a mistake but she's clearly manipulated the lyrics vengefully the second time.

Although she shares the stage with her children, with everyone singing and enjoying each other's company, at the end of the show when Judy sings "Over the Rainbow," you can feel the same uncomfortable feeling, much like the opening in "Have Yourself a Merry Little Christmas." Judy has to belt out another of her signature songs, which undermines the small, intimate moment she's sharing with her children. However, even when Judy isn't at her best, she's still better than most. This explains why her Christmas special remains a very popular vintage favorite.

The Ed Sullivan Show offered Christmas entertainment that few series could rival. Each year there could be an angelic children's choir from a European mountain community, followed by a trained dog act, an award winning Broadway singer performing a religious carol, an attention-getting stand-up comic reworking "Twas the Night Before Christmas," and of course, the little puppet mouse, the Italian Topo Gigio in a Christmas fantasy. Once you've seen the performance, you'll never forget the elegance of the Supremes in 1966, with Diana Ross in front. Dressed in flowing pink, chiffon gowns, the girls turn the familiar tune of "My Favorite Things" into their own, original sounding Supremes' song—all on a stage decorated in tall columns of shiny wrapped Christmas packages. The 1953 appearance of the precocious country-western singer, Little Jimmy Boyd singing his singular version of "I Saw Mommy Kissing Santa Claus" is equally memorable. The early 1950's holiday performance of Spanish ventriloquist Señor Wences holding three conversations at once between Johnny his boy puppet, Pedro the disembodied head in a box and Santa Claus, is also likely to etch itself on your mind.

The Frank Sinatra Show, the superstar's second attempt at success with his own TV show, produced an amazing 1957 Christmas chapter. With a host like Sinatra, what guest star could possibly impress as much as Old Blue Eyes himself? None other than Mr. Christmas himself, Bing Crosby. When the episode begins, the Chairman of the Board is in a quintessential 1950s home setting, supposedly decorating his Christmas tree, when his good friend Bing Crosby casually drops by the Sinatra bachelor pad for a

Photo: *Bing Crosby and Frank Sinatra on* ***The Frank Sinatra Show*** *(1957).*

Photofest/American Broadcasting Company (ABC)

jovial Christmas sing-along. The "friends" sing a jazzy duet of "Jingle Bells" before slipping into Victorian costume to join carolers singing door-to-door in Ye Old English town. Near the end, both men gather by the fireplace together to sing "The Christmas Song" before they sit down to a sumptuous Christmas dinner. It is truly too much TV goodness crammed into one special.

It became an annual TV tradition for variety show hosts to invite their family members onto their Christmas shows. Sometimes these show biz relatives would even sing, dance or play an instrument for the TV family watching. For example, starting in 1966, Bing Crosby began to invite his young wife Kathryn and their three children, Mary Frances, Nathaniel and Harry on his Christmas shows year after year. With each new Christmas special, TV viewers watched their favorite star's children grow up. One hilarious family moment came on live TV during an episode of *The Ford Show* and is included in the PBS-produced clip show, *A Tennessee Ernie Ford Family Christmas*. While Ford tenderly sings "Children Go Where I Send Thee" with the casts' children quietly gathered around his feet, Ford's own young son begins to imitate the singer, upstaging his performance! Another child, disturbed by the son's antics, looks straight into the camera and makes a "crazy" gesture, while a third child literally stands up and walks off stage! Ford and his back up singers all begin laughing in the middle of the song during this live TV moment.

Young Mary Frances Crosby eventually grew up to become an actress, playing Kristen on ***Dallas****, the role that captured audiences' utmost attention in 1980 when the question "Who Shot J.R.?" was finally answered.*

Variety Jumps the Shark

By the 1970s, variety shows had saturated the ever-changing appetites of television viewers. Those variety programs that remained on the air struggled to even greater lengths to keep viewers. But this desperation produced some great television moments. One such moment is often featured in clips on TV specials created about Christmas specials, from the 1976 holiday show of *Captain and Tennille*. In truly one of the must be seen to be believed segments, the show opens with Toni singing a latin-inspired version of "Jingle Bells" dressed as a Christmas Carmen Miranda, as she and Daryl enter the stage, riding atop a red, zamboni-like, motorized organ. They just don't make 'em like this anymore!

When TV viewers watch entertainers' families year after year at Christmas, it often feels like these people too become a part of our own families. This sentiment caused quite a scandal in 1976 when Andy Williams' former wife, French actress and singer, Claudine Longet, was arrested for fatally shooting her boyfriend, Olympic skier, Vladmir "Spider" Sabich, in Aspen Colorado. Though Williams had finalized their divorce the previous year, he publicly stood by the mother of his three children through her trial, which resulted in her conviction on the charge of misdemeanor criminal negligence.

1976 also gave us an incredibly bizarre retelling of Dickens' *A Christmas Carol* in a comedy sketch from *The Sonny and Cher Show*. In the reoccurring skit about the Italian restaurant, "Sonny's Pizza," the staff of the greasy spoon complain about the business being open on Christmas Eve and Christmas day. Business owner Sonny falls asleep and experiences a dream in which he's visited by three ghostly pizzas encouraging him to change his scrooge-like ways. Though Sonny and the other actors are clearly in the know, with tongues firmly planted in cheeks, it's still an unbelievable moment. Cher plays the Ghost of Pizzas Past, Captain Kangaroo/Bob Keeshan plays the flying Ghost of Pizzas Present and Bernadette Peters plays the Ghost of Pizzas Yet To Come before Sonny has his inevitable change of heart. Sonny throws his employees, Rosa and Luigi, a Christmas dinner celebration by ordering out for pizza.

Airing originally on Canadian TV in 1978 and later on HBO, is the reference-saturated *Rich Little's A Christmas Carol*, a TV special sure to please any pop culture junky. Master impressionist Rich Little plays all the roles in this unique version of Dickens' classic. However, this comedy adaptation is even more special because Little adds another layer of cultural meaning to each of the roles, that is, playing Ebenezer Scrooge with the voice of the cantankerous hard-drinking W. C. Fields, Bob Cratchit as the put-upon Paul Lynde, and Jacob Marley as the regretful Richard Nixon. Little plays the Ghost of Christmas Past as tough talking Humphrey Bogart; the Ghost of Christmas Present is the voice of Peter Falk as his rumpled detective Columbo, and the Ghost of Christmas Future is the voice of Peter Sellers as the clumsy Inspector Clouseau. Other personalities include: Johnny Carson, Laurel and Hardy, Groucho Marx, Jimmy Stewart, Edith Bunker, Truman Capote, John Wayne, George Burns, James Mason, Jack Benny and Dean Martin.

*Rich Little made an appearance on a Christmas episode of the **Ed Sullivan Show** in the 1960s, performing a similar pastiche of personalities in a truncated retelling of **A Christmas Carol**. Then, he used the voice of penny-pinching, Jack Benny as the character of Scrooge, the voice of Ed Sullivan as the Ghost of Christmas Past and George Burns as the story's narrator.*

Although the overly familiar story of *A Christmas Carol* is nothing new at holiday time, this version of it will easily hold your attention as you listen closely to identify which cleverly chosen voice Little adds to his cast of characters. My personal favorite is the hilariousness of watching Little play the character Tiny Tim as Truman Capote.

A particularly cheesy legacy has been bequeathed by the Christmas installments of the hits list makers of the 1980s, *Solid Gold*. The program annually entitled their yuletide episode "A Solid Gold Christmas," typically counting down the forty most popular Christmas songs, and featuring entertainers singing these chestnuts, or featuring the barely clad Solid Gold Dancers gyrating to a popular recording of the hit. Considering that the series concerned itself with counting down the popular music of the day, it was off-putting that the celebrity guests on the Christmas specials usually didn't have a current youth market hit. So Dionne Warwick sings a disco arrangement of "Rockin' Around the Christmas Tree;" John Davidson sings "Have Yourself a Merry Little Christmas," and Crystal Gayle sings "Silver Bells"—despite their absence from any youth market music charts. Even more campy are the Solid Gold Dancers bumping and grinding every year to a rhythm and blues arrangement, recorded by Elvis Presley in 1971, of "Merry Christmas Baby." Equally ridiculous is the country and western barn dance to John Denver's 1975 hit "Christmas for Cowboys," complete with cowboy boots, hats and suede, fringy vests. When it aired, this show was out of step with the charting hits and the youth market of its day, but now, more than twenty years later, this museum piece is truly a sight to behold.

*In the 1981 **SCTV** episode "SCTV Staff Christmas Party" there's a spot-on parody of the Solid Gold dancers in the segment entitled "The Dusty Towne Sexy Holiday Special." Andrea Martin portrays Solid Gold dancer, Marcie Odette, as a special guest on "Dusty Towne's Christmas Show," prancing vulgarly to a synthesized music version of "Frosty the Snowman." The parody captures the real Solid Gold dancers so perfectly that there's not much exaggeration needed.*

Classic Christmas Variety Parodies

Along with the sincere Christmas musical spectaculars of the golden age of TV, the industry has also created a collection of parodies. The most noteworthy parodies not only make fun of the excesses and obvious contrivances of Christmases past, but often serve as homages to the old shows as well.

A favorite is the 1988 *Pee-Wee's Playhouse Christmas Special* that not only reminds us of the corny spectacles of an earlier era but also honors and outshines some of the best of them! First of all, the list of guest stars is dizzying and overwhelming, including Oprah Winfrey, Dinah Shore, Cher, Magic Johnson, Joan Rivers, kd lang, Whoopi Goldberg and Little Richard. There are also amazing guest stars that reflect Pee-Wee's unique style too, such as Annette Funicello, Frankie Avalon, the Del Rubio Triplets, Charo, and Zsa Zsa Gabor. If your mind is not blown yet, he also hosts musical guest Grace Jones in all her weirdness, performing a shocking version of "The Little Drummer Boy" as she bursts from a special delivery, life-sized wooden crate, addressed to the Playhouse. Some celebrities perform: kd lang sings "Jingle Bell Rock," Charo sings

"Feliz Navidad," and the Del Rubio Triplets sing "Winter Wonderland." The fun of this special is seeing the celebrities drop by the Playhouse to participate in the holiday fun: Cher asks Conky for the word of the day; Magic Johnson plays along with Magic Screen; Little Richard ice skates on the frozen pond outside; and Frankie and Annette slavishly make Pee-Wee's Christmas cards all by hand. Others such as Oprah and Whoopi Goldberg appear only in video-phone conversations to express their holiday greetings. Dinah Shore sings an endless version of "The Twelve Days of Christmas" while an annoyed Pee-Wee steps away from the phone. But Pee-Wee welcomes each of his guests as well as his regular cast, such as Miss Yvonne, Jambi, Cowboy Curtis, Reba and the King of Cartoons—all despite the fact that each brings the same unwanted gift: a brick of fruitcake.

The animated segment shown by the King of Cartoons is the classic Fleischer Studios, 1936, ***Christmas Comes But Once a Year*** *featuring the elderly inventor Grampy, a reoccurring character originally introduced in a Betty Boop cartoon.*

Another comic triumph is a sketch from *SCTV* starring series regular, Dave Thomas, as the piano-playing showman of Las Vegas in "Liberace's Musical Tribute to the Holidays" seen on the 1981 episode "SCTV Staff Christmas Party." Rick Moranis plays Liberace's special guest, the flamboyant, Elton John as the two sound off in a dueling pianos bit on "Carol of the Bells." Don't miss Thomas as Liberace playing the song "Sleigh Ride" while a buff Santa cracks a whip in time to the music next to him. To appreciate how dead-on Thomas' Liberace character actually is, look for the 1954 Christmas episode of *The Liberace Show*. The charming showman is at his best during his performance of "Sleigh Ride" where his white grand piano continuously rotates in a full circle while he plays. And then he winks into the camera!

The network known for broadcasting old reruns late into the night, Nick @ Nite, produced its own original program in 2003 entitled "The Nick at Nite Holiday Special." This is a parody of an old fashioned variety show Christmas special, crammed with sitcom stars and hit recording artists. A blizzard is brewing and the Nick At Nite Lodge is staying open for business on Christmas Eve. The lodge is staffed by innkeeper Martin Mull, housekeeper Joyce DeWitt, baker Jackée Harry, ski instructor John Schneider and bellboy French Stewart. Celebrity musical guests check in to the lodge throughout the evening to seek shelter from the storm and to perform for the gathering guests. A partial list of stars includes Chaka Khan, Lil' Romeo, Amy Grant and Vince Gill, Natalie Cole, Clay Aiken and Sarah McLachlan.

The stand out moment is clearly the Clay Aiken duet with Bing Crosby on "The Little Drummer Boy/Peace on Earth." This number begs for a comparison to the original duet between David Bowie and Bing Crosby from Crosby's 1977 Christmas special. Your age may determine whether you think the new pairing of the *American Idol* runner-up and the legendary singer is awesome or awful. I've always felt the original duo's wow factor lay in the juxtaposition of mainstream Crosby's acceptability with Bowie's incredible reputation for boundary pushing. This new pairing seems disappointing because Aiken's career lacks a propensity for experimentation, thus the Christmas moment lacks the original duet's excitement. Also, the special effects used to resurrect Crosby make the singer look more like an animated creature than a truly lifelike memory. I found more emotional satisfaction in Natalie Cole's performance of "The Christmas Song," a holiday tradition made popular by a famous recording by her late father, Nat "King" Cole. This more subdued musical performance actually has the sentimental power behind it that the contrived Crosby moment lacks.

There's also 2005's *Denis Leary's Merry F#%$in' Christmas Special.* There's nothing sentimental in this spoof of the familiar, sappy, celebrity-filled Christmas special, and the attitude is much darker here—exactly what you'd expect from the foul-mouthed, hilarious, chain-smoking, stand-up comedian. You can tell from the twisted images and the hostile theme tune lyrics in the opening segment: a claymation tribute to the Rankin/Bass *Rudolph* special—complete with an animated, singing Leary—that this isn't your typical nostalgic, wholesome TV special. The first segment is "Christmas with Mr. Shatner" where William Shatner gathers a group of children to mock sad and tragic letters to Santa written by poor children. The actor also coaches the children on how to ply Santa with fourteen year-old scotch and Cuban cigars to get the best Christmas presents. The rest of the comedy sketches follow in a similar tone, occasionally sinking into mean-spiritedness. Highlights include: Carmen Electra delivers a parody charity appeal: "Tits for Tots;" an animated parody of *A Charlie Brown Christmas* with Charlie losing his faith in Christianity; actor/writer Chris Elliot serves as a war correspondent to bring holiday greetings to the troops in Grenada; a parody commercial starring Billy Dee Williams for "Colt 45D," a malt liquor cold medicine; Leary discusses violent Christmas toy presents from his youth and their ability to teach kids to live smarter (or thin the herd); and documentary filmmaker Morgan Spurlock tests his sanity by watching the 1988 made-for-TV movie *A Very Brady Christmas* twice a day for 30 days straight. Despite the latest trend of TV Christmas specials that are deliberately offensive, mocking and ironically funny, this is the harshest of them all. It's also the funniest—even if you're laughing because you're uncomfortable or you can't believe that Leary pushes it as far as he does.

Animator Corky Quakenbush created the opening segment—a stop motion animation short with Denis Leary singing the show's theme song. Quakenbush is also responsible for creating the animated "The Reinfather" and "Ragin' Rudolph," which are discussed in the Animation Chapter on pages 83-84.).

Another amusing parody comes from the children's animated series *The Replacements,* with the 2008 episode, "Dick Daring's All-Star Holiday Stunt Spectacular." Stuntman Dick Daring hosts a musical variety Christmas TV special with stunts, music and dancing. His daughter, Riley, acts as back stage director and son, Todd, is a telethon fundraiser for call-in charity donations. Sketches reference the 1960's classic *Rowan and Martin's Laugh-In* and more recent practical joke-centered series. Special animated guests include quarterback Carson Palmer, actor Josh Duhamel and environmentalist/actor Ed Begley Jr. who repeatedly walks on stage and delivers the message, "Have a Carbon Neutral Holiday!" It's a clever concept for an animated program—a special Christmas variety show complete with celebrity guests, sketch comedy, music and live audience noises. It's an interesting nod to the classic holiday programming made popular in the 1960s—clearly beyond the experience of the average ten year-old viewer.

The Greatest of Them All

Who says they don't make fun, star-studded musical Christmas specials any more? 2008 also gave us *A Colbert Christmas: The Greatest Gift of All!* Here, Stephen Colbert is trapped in his panel-lined, rustic cabin by a wild, hungry bear. He is unable to leave to get to the studio to tape his Christmas Special but is visited by friends and visions. In this hilarious spoof, Colbert alludes to the popular Christmas specials from the past. There are celebrity friends who drop by his "home," as well as elaborate sets and costumes. Highlights include: Elvis Costello dressed as a toy soldier and jack-in-the-box. Colbert awkwardly catches each of his guests under the mistletoe and expects a kiss. Willie Nelson appears as a figurine in Colbert's Nativity set, and

John Stewart makes a humorous plea for Hanukkah. John Legend, as the forest ranger, drops by and sings a naughty song about nutmeg, while Feist appears as the angel on the top of Colbert's Christmas tree. Elvis Costello, dressed as a Dickens' character, gets eaten by the bear, and the entire cast comes together to sing "(What's So Funny About) Peace, Love and Understanding." George Wendt makes a special appearance as Santa Claus, cutting the bear open to release the previously eaten Costello and to give Colbert the only gift he wants: his Christmas Special.

A favorite moment: Willie Nelson's original song is a send up of "The Little Drummer Boy" with Colbert singing the harmony part, ala Bing Crosby and David Bowie's now-famous duet. That alone is funny but the lyrics are about giving the gift of marijuana to the baby Jesus! And later, Nelson as the figurine is caught in a drug bust at the stable.

Ding Dong Merrily on High: Special Musical Guests

Special appearances by musical guests are to be expected at holiday time just as the incorporation of a musical portion into a series, such as a sitcom or a drama, can also be found throughout television. For example, the family sitcom, *The Brady Bunch* includes a musical segment in its 1969 "The Voice of Christmas" episode when Carol Brady, played by Florence Henderson, sings "O Come All Ye Faithful" in church. However, some performances are more noteworthy than others.

Mr. Las Vegas, Wayne Newton appears the 1966 episode of *Bonanza* entitled "A Christmas Story" singing "Home Is Where I Want to Be on Christmas." He also duets with Ben Cartwright, played by Lorne Greene, singing "Silent Night." Another singer, Broadway sensation, Robert Goulet, appears in a holiday episode of *Two Guys, A Girl and A Pizza Place* in 1999's "Out With the Old." Invited to Ashley's New Year's Eve party, Goulet appears as himself and spends the evening hogging the karaoke machine. Goulet also does voice work in a Christmas episode of the animated *Disney's Recess* from 1998 called "Yes Mikey, Santa Does Shave" The young Mikey's singing (provided by Goulet) is so mature and professional, he is asked to play the lead in the school's holiday pageant.

In a 1997 episode of *Sabrina the Teenage Witch* entitled "Sabrina Claus," the young witch wants to recapture the feeling of her Christmases past so she uses her magic to zap Johnny Mathis himself into her home to sing his classics, "Winter Wonderland" and "O Holy Night." And, legend Rosemary Clooney plays Madame X/Mary Cavanaugh, the Alzheimer's patient on the medical drama, *ER*, who anonymously roams the halls of the hospital in 1994's "The Gift," beautifully singing familiar carols.

Actress/singer Rosemary Clooney was one of the co-stars of the classic holiday film, 1954's ***White Christmas*** *which also featured Bing Crosby and Danny Kaye.*

Aerosmith front man Steven Tyler appears as himself on the 2002 "Xtreme Xmas" episode of *Lizzie McGuire* on a holiday parade float singing "Santa Claus is Coming to Town." Tyler's real-life kids, Chelsea and Taj Tallirico appear as well, as parade bystanders.

George Michael appears on the 2007 Christmas show of *The Catherine Tate Show* as himself in a comedy sketch with regular character, nurse Bernie. She discovers that the pop star is a patient in hospital on her ward and won't give him any privacy. Eventually, we see him singing a duet with Bernie at the hospital staff Christmas karaoke party! They sing the much beloved "Fairytale of New York" popularized by the Irish band, The Pogues featuring Kristy MacColl.

Ludicris appears in the theatrical release, 2007's *Fred Claus* as the diminutive elf, DJ Donnie who pushes title character Fred, played by Vince Vaughn, close to the edge of insanity by insisting on only playing the song "Here Comes Santa Claus" throughout the toy factory.

The 1988 movie *Scrooged* also includes several hip musicians: David Johansen from the legendary glam band, the New York Dolls plays the taxi-driving, Ghost of Christmas Past. Jazz fans can spot Miles Davis playing "We Three Kings" on his trumpet in a very brief scene with street musicians, alongside saxophonist David Sanborn, keyboardist Paul Shaffer and guitarist Larry Carlton.

Making Spirits Bright: Regular Cast Musical Surprises

Medical detective show *Crossing Jordan* star, actress Jill Hennessy surprises many when she appears playing an acoustic guitar and singing The Pretenders' holiday standard, "2000 Miles" in the 2001 episode "Blue Christmas." Obviously, the actress is also an accomplished musical talent.

In the 1964 rebroadcast of the 1956 episode, "Busy Christmas," from *The Adventures of Ozzie and Harriet,* a musical segment is added to the end of the story to include heartthrob Ricky Nelson singing the sentimental favorite "The Christmas Song." Rick appears with his wife, Kris and their young baby, Tracy Nelson—who went on to become a successful actress in her own right. My favorite role of Tracy's is that of the popular girl, Jennifer DiNuccio, on the early '80's teen series *Square Pegs.*

Another unusual Christmas TV moment occurs on *The Monkees'* 1967 "Christmas Show." With Mickey Dolenz as lead vocalist, the TV band harmonizes a hauntingly beautiful acappella version of "Riu Chiu." However, what's not explained is that this is an ancient liturgical song from the 16th century Spain, sung in the original Spanish and a standard in Christmas musical performances of

Renaissance-era Christian church music, (also sometimes called "Riu Riu Chiu"). Who knew *The Monkees,* a show known for its pop musical performances, was capable of honoring such high, cultural traditions?

Kids' Christmas: Unreal Rock 'n Roll Special Guests

Even children's shows offer unusual musical guests, as can be seen in the 2007 "Christmas" episode of the surreal program for preschoolers, *Yo Gabba Gabba.* Musician and composer Mark Mothersbaugh demonstrates how to draw a snowman. Mothersbaugh is widely known as a member of the 1980's band with a philosophy, Devo, as well as his more recent work composing music for TV shows and films.

A more mainstream hit, *Dora the Explorer* recruited Backstreet Boy Howie Dorough to voice the character of Santa Claus in the 2001 episode "A Present for Santa." Dorough sings the Latin classic "Feliz Navidad" with the perky, map-clutching, animated Dora.

My favorite kids show Christmas musical performance comes from the painful-to-watch-for-adults, *The Wiggles.* In 2004's "Santa's Rockin" episode, the exuberant Aussies entertain preschoolers with song and dance, and they invite special guest Barry Williams to join them on the original tune, "Wags Stop Your Barking, It's Almost Christmas Day!" The actor/singer who started his career playing Greg Brady on *The Brady Bunch* in the late 1960s is surely under-appreciated by the toddler viewers the program is aimed at. That same episode also includes Rock and Roll Hall of Famer, John Fogerty, though he's overshadowed by the surreal appearance of the original Johnny Bravo.

Hidden Gems: High Class Nut Cracking

For those cult TV watchers who also have cultivated the high art tastes to include performances of *The Nutcracker,* I recommend the outstanding, highly stylized interpretation of the traditional ballet entitled *The Hard Nut,* choreographed by Mark Morris for the Mark Morris Dance Group in the Theatre Royal de la Monnaie, in Brussels. Though the Tchaikovsky music and two part structure remains traditional, everything else about this adaptation is unique. The production design is courtesy of illustrator/comics artist Charles Burns, well-known for his artwork for Seattle's independent record label Sub Pop, as well as Iggy Pop's *Brick By Brick* album cover, and Burns' own comics.

The Hard Nut is no longer set in the nineteenth century, but updated to the 1960s-'70s with very modern sensibilities. Act I contains the Christmas party. Drosselmeier gives Marie the nutcracker that her brother breaks, and a battle between the toys results in the defeat of the Rat King. Act II breaks even further from tradition—there is no Sugar Plum Fairy or Kingdom of Sweets. Instead there is a fairy tale about a rat's curse on a beautiful princess and an international journey for the magical cure which ends in true love for the suitor who can break the hard nut. The performance closes with a final love dance between Marie and her transformed prince. Much about *The Hard Nut* embraces more modern attitudes. The typical gendered roles for the dancers are expanded to include both genders—not just background dancers but major female parts are played by men. And once in love, Marie is exposed to a Waltz of the Flowers—a beautiful fertility dance—a natural rite endorsed by her mother. But the highlight for non-tradi-

***Photo**: Eric Burdon and the Animals with Cyril Ritchard in **The Dangerous Christmas of Red Riding Hood** (1965).*

ABC/Photofest

tionalists is the striking production design. In Act I, the combination of black and white, modern set with stylized costumes adding color, and the wonderful illustration style from Charles Burns permeates the ever-changing sets. This is much cooler, hipper and quirkier than any other version of *The Nutcracker*. The dance performance also comes the closest to the original early nineteenth century Hoffman text. *The Hard Nut* includes an adaptation of the story of Princess Pirlipat, an element of the original story ignored by the traditional ballet.

Hark! The Herald Angels Sing: Broadway-style Variety Spectaculars

It is also a TV Christmas tradition to watch live-action, Broadway-style stage productions of children's fairy tales such as Pinocchio and ballet performances of *Sleeping Beauty*. One noteworthy production that actually includes a reference to Christmas is *The Dangerous Christmas of Red Riding Hood* from 1965. Subtitled "Oh Wolf, Poor Wolf," this is a live-action retelling of the classic fairy tale, "Little Red Riding Hood" from the perspective of the wolf. Teenager Liza Minnelli stars as Red Riding Hood, crooner Vic Damone as the Woodsman, Cyril Ritchard as Lone T. Wolf and British rockers, Eric Burdon and the Animals appear as the wild Wolf Pack. This updated story begins with Wolf behind bars trying to explain his innocence. He insists his good intentioned attempt at making friends with Miss Hood was mistaken for a less civilized act of aggression. But Wolf becomes jealous of her instant attraction to the woodchopper and he poses as her granny to get closer to her. Original music for this TV special was written by Jule Styne and Bob Merrill, who earned their reputation on Broadway. Eric Burdon and the Animals have several musical numbers. Look for "We're Gonna Howl Tonight" which features the British Invasion favorites with their rock instruments, playing a song closer to their own style.

*Jule Styne and Bob Merrill also created the music for the Broadway show within the cartoon, **Mr. Magoo's Christmas Carol**. Styne paired with Sammy Cahn to write the music for the 1970 animated classic, **The Night the Animals Talked**, as well as the classic songs "Let It Snow, Let It Snow, Let It Snow" and "The Christmas Waltz."*

A Contemporary Classic

There's also the much overlooked concert performance of contemporary musicians in the 2004 original program made by BET, called *Christmas Memories*. This Christmas concert offers holiday music from the hottest recording artists, including: John Legend singing "Oh, Holy Night" and "What a Wonderful Child;" Avant doing "Christmas Came to the Ghetto" and "Give Love on Christmas Day;" Faith Evans performing "Merry Christmas, Baby" and "This Christmas;" Wyclef Jean playing "The Little Drummer Boy" and "Feliz Navidad;" and Keyshia Cole singing

"Silent Night." Make sure to hear the reggae version of "The Little Drummer Boy" by Wyclef Jean, whose arrangement breathes new life and spirit into the familiar tune. Between the performances are short interview segments with various celebrities sharing their own Christmas memories. Skip the popular but predictable musical concert performances on the annual *Christmas in Rockefeller Center* and the like to look for this virtually ignored TV special which contains wonderfully sincere performances and unique arrangements.

MYOM:
Blue Christmas

Elvis Presley has long been associated with the holiday season through his iconic interpretations of hit songs such as "Blue Christmas" and "Merry Christmas Baby." Elvis' numerous successful gospel recordings also closely tie him to this religious holiday for many people as well. His landmark TV special *Elvis,* also known as the *'68 Comeback Special,* was broadcast in December of that year, further cementing him to the holiday television experience. Because of this close association, many programs pay homage to the original King of Rock n' Roll by incorporating his music or character into their holiday material.

TV junkies may already be familiar with Fes' Elvis impersonation in the 2003 episode "Christmas" of *That '70s Show.* At the school dance, the foreign exchange student tries to liven the event when he jumps on stage to sing "Blue Christmas." In the 2000 holiday episode, "The Christmas Present," on *Everybody Loves Raymond,* Ray Barone can be seen vacuuming the floor around the tree on Christmas morning comically warbling "In the Ghetto," a song long associated with Elvis.

Another holiday Elvis sighting is the 2006 episode of *Las Vegas* entitled "White Christmas." The Montecido casino hosts a special exhibit of the King of Rock n' Roll memorabilia over the holiday, so Christmas songs by Elvis can be heard playing throughout the casino and as intro and outro music between commercial breaks.

A rare moment in the history of television takes place in *A Johnny Cash Christmas* special from 1979. Guest, comedian Andy Kaufman takes the opportunity to perform his incredible, dead-on impersonation of Elvis, singing "That's When Your Heartaches Begin." Kaufman cultivated a reputation for blurring the line between humor and seriousness when he entertained and this is unquestionably one of those moments when he is clearly paying an authentic tribute to the King.

But the most touching Christmas tribute to Elvis was created by the people that knew him. On the 1977 *Johnny Cash Christmas Special*, Johnny and his guests Carl Perkins, Roy Orbison and Jerry Lee Lewis pay special homage to the then recently deceased Presley and fellow Sun Studios recording artist. The four legends sing the gospel hit "This Train Is Bound for Glory" in honor of the man they knew who had just died that previous August.

MYOM: THE 12 DAYS OF CULT TV CHRISTMAS—Part 1

This holiday don't concern yourself with gathering together all those birds, golden rings, ladies dancing, lords a-leaping, et al. Instead, spend your twelve days watching the Christmas episodes of your favorite cult TV shows. The following cult shows are ones not already mentioned elsewhere in this book and are provided to help you arrange your own holiday viewing schedule. A TV junky will be familiar with these programs. However, do you remember the holiday episodes?

12. **Have Yourself a Supermarionation Christmas.** There are three Christmas episodes of the Gerry Anderson-produced, futuristic shows from the 1960s. In *Stingray*'s 1964 episode "A Christmas To Remember," Troy Tempest and Atlanta arrange for a young orphan boy, Barry, to visit Marineville at Christmas. But Tempest is distracted by a captured sub that appears to be crewless. During a re-creation of the attack to determine whether or not the enemy crew had a chance to escape, Troy asks the young Barry to accompany him on his Stingray submarine. When the unseen enemy reappears, Barry is in the right place to assist his hero Troy on an unexpected adventure to capture them. It's an underwater Christmas experience he'll never forget.

In the 1966 *Thunderbirds*' episode, "Give or Take a Million," the father of the Tracy clan explains the events of the last several days to a little boy named Nicky, from the children's hospital. Harman's department store arranged for a toy drop-off for the children at Coralville Hospital for Christmas. One of the gifts in the donation was a special surprise for one lucky child: an opportunity to spend Christmas day with International Rescue. But the canister filled with the toys to be delivered by a rocket ship also contains two stowaways dressed as Father Christmas—two unfortunate robbers trying to evade capture for breaking into the Second

National Bank. Brains spends Christmas Eve, deep in research, in order to find a way to make it snow on the Tracy private tropical island—natural climate, be damned! If you look closely, you can identify several Hanna-Barbera and Walt Disney licensed toys for sale at Harman's.

Also not to be missed is the 1968 episode of *Joe 90*, entitled "The Unorthodox Shepherd." Here, choir practice for Christmas is sparsely attended because the locals think the church is haunted due to strange noises, unexplainable movements and mysterious bell ringing. Joe recognizes that the dollar bill the vicar gave him is a forgery, printed from original plates supposedly destroyed years ago. Mac and Sam learn that the forgers are working in a mausoleum in the church's cemetery and decide to spook them out. Sam pretends that he's the voice of the deceased occupant of the mausoleum that the counterfeiters' printing press inhabits, while Joe, dressed as an avenging angel, flies through the air, haunting the forgers from beyond the grave to change their ways!

Fandersons (fans of Gerry Anderson-produced TV series) may also want to check out the Supermacromation series, *Terrahawks*' 1983 holiday episode, "A Christmas Miracle." Here, the ever-vigilant, Tiger Ninestein anticipates that the android villain Zelda will attack on Christmas day in an attempt to find the defense taskforce unprepared. Their fleet gets in position on the Moon and the massive battle begins. In the spirit of the season, Captains Mary and Kate put an end to the volley of bombardments, asking androids Cy-Star and Yung-Star to join them in the Spacehawk space station for a Christmas party with music and dancing.

In this episode, Yung-Star's Kaiser Wilhelm helmet must surely be a reference to the Christmas truce of WWI—a real-life spontaneous cease fire during the fierceness of battle between the Germans and the French and British troops. I ask you, what could be better than a puppet-centric start to Christmas?

11. Share a Kiss With Emma Peel Under the Mistletoe. A black-and-white episode of *The Avengers* classic "Too Many Christmas Trees" from 1965 sees John Steed feeling uneasy after experiencing a week's worth of disturbing Christmas nightmares. So Peel invites him to join her in attending a Dickens-themed masquerade over the holiday. Here Steed finds the origin of his Christmas dreams in a group conducting psychic experiments, infiltrating and influencing his behavior through his bizarre dreams. He and Peel fight off a masked, murderous Father Christmas in a room full of mirrors, foiling another plot to steal state secrets. Note their costumes: Emma is dressed as Oliver Twist while Steed is Sydney Carton from *A Tale of Two Cities*.

There's also the 1963 New Year's episode entitled "Dressed to Kill" where Steed is invited to a New Year's Eve costume party aboard a train. Suspicious of the invitation, Steed, dressed as a cowboy invites Cathy Gale to trail him. She does, cunningly hidden under monk's robes. Sure enough, the party guests are left stranded in the club car at a deserted train station. They soon determine that the only thing they have in common is an appointment to purchase a parcel of land at an auction the following day. While they figure out that they are being prevented from making the purchases, they also begin accusing each other for the responsibility for the kidnapping. Could it be the policeman, the archer, Napoleon, or the pussy cat?

Avengers fans will also be familiar with 1969's episode "Take-Over." With Tara on her own vacation, Steed heads to the country to visit friends and partake of the relaxing activities of country living, such as hunting and enjoying good food and drink. He's expected by his friend because they reunite each February to celebrate Christmas—an annual tradition, Steed explains, ever since Steed and he were prisoners in China. They had made their own calendar and later found that they had over-calculated the date, and had been celebrating the holiday in February. But Steed's

Christmas reunion is not to be when he discovers strangers occupying his friend's home, holding him hostage with a devious scheme in mind. Of course, Steed cleverly fakes his own death, appearing to drown in a mud pit. What latest plot to alter the world's course is being enacted at his friend's home?

10. Laugh Yourself Silly in Victorian Times. In *Blackadder's Christmas Carol,* Ebenezer Blackadder is the kindest, most generous man in nineteenth century England. But when the Ghost of Christmas Past visits him and shows him visions of his conniving ancestors, he has a change of heart and decides to pursue the earthly rewards of a villainous lifestyle! This reverse *Christmas Carol* is brilliant.

9. Macy's Department Store Almost Brings Down Communism. On the 1966 *The Man from U.N.C.L.E.* episode "The Jingle Bells Affair," Solo and Kuryakin are in charge of providing security to the Russian Chairman who is scheduled to speak at the United Nations over the holiday. But his Russian comrades fear that the Chairman will become so enamored by what he sees at the lavish American department store that he will betray the Communist commitment.

8. Portrayals of Winter Celebrations Past—Way, Way Past. There are two Christmas episodes one each set in the ancient, mythic times of *Hercules: The Legendary Journeys* and *Xena: Warrior Princess.* In 1996's "A Star to Guide Them," Hercules' partner, Iolaus, joins three men who are journeying to a northern land where a king is killing newborn infants in order to protect his reign. In 1996's campy episode, "A Solstice Carol," Xena disguises herself as the Three Fates to teach a greedy king a lesson. Meanwhile, Gabrielle helps inspire a former toy maker to dress in a red suit and distribute gifts to children in an orphanage. What next, a *Lord of the Rings* Yuletide?

For completists: *Xena* fans will remember the attempt at a spin-off series, *Cleopatra 2525,* starring actress Gina Torres. This series features a Christmas episode, entitled "Choices," from 2000.

7. Irwin Allen's Adventure Christmases. In 1965, on *Lost in Space*'s "Return from Outer Space," Will Robinson travels back to Earth briefly at Christmas to retrieve a chemical to help his family preserve their food and continue to survive in space. And, 1969's *Land of the Giants*' episode "Night of Thrombeldinbar" sees tiny Fitzhugh mistaken for the planet's cookie-eating, holiday elf.

Nutty as a Fruitcake: Outrageous Animation

THIS CHAPTER IS UNLIKE ANY OF THE OTHERS which are collections of Christmas materials based on genres or themes. Here, the focus is on animation—a form of storytelling that spans all genres and themes. Although I have included animated material in the other chapters, this chapter, "Nutty as a Fruitcake: Outrageous Animation" focuses on the most cutting-edge and provocative Christmas installments of animated television programs.

Honoring History

Regardless of our different religious, ethnic, and family Christmas traditions, we all have watched these three animated television specials: 1964's *Rudolph the Red-Nosed Reindeer*, 1965's *A Charlie Brown Christmas* and 1966's *How the Grinch Stole Christmas!* Even though the network and creative expectations for the low budget, animated specials were modest during their initial release, these programs have grown to become the standards against which all other holiday programs have been viewed. Much Christmas material parodies these animated classics; these are a few that are among the more mind-blowing.

Rankin/Bass-mas

The best parodies of the Rankin/Bass Animagic special *Rudolph the Red-Nosed Reindeer* have appeared as sketches on *Mad TV*. In the mid-90's, *Mad TV* broadcast "Raging

Rudolph" on their Christmas show which retold the familiar tale as if it were an Italian gangster film directed by Martin Scorsese, referring to *Goodfellas* and even *Taxi Driver*. Rudolph wants to be one of Santa's "made" reindeer, so he teams up with Hermey "The Drill." Together, they enlist the help of Yukon Corneleone and they put a hit on Santa. In 2006, *MadTV* followed this with a sequel "The Reinfather," this time with the same *Rudolph* characters paying homage to *The Godfather*. Don Rudolph makes an elf an offer he can't refuse by putting a polar bear head into his bed, and Yukon Brazzi gets pumped full of lead when his dog sled stops at a toll booth, just like the original death scene of Sonny Corleone. Both uproariously funny stop motion segments were made by Corky Quackenbush. It seems to me the streets of the North Pole are mean ones, indeed.

*Several TV series have paid homage to the Rankin/Bass Animagic specials by incorporating an Animagic-style animated segment into a holiday episode. A 1996 Thanksgiving episode, **Home Improvement's** "The Wood, The Bad and the Hungry" sees Tool Man, Tim Taylor dreaming he's a character in an Animagic special. 2001's **That '70s Show's** "An Eric Forman Christmas" features an animated Kelso, and **George Lopez's** 2005 "George is Being Elfish and Christ-Misses His Family" depicts George as a big-headed, depressed elf that misses his family.*

The Charlie Browniest Christmas

A fantastic animated spin-off from the Charles Schultz cartoon is "A Huey Freeman Christmas" from the 2005 series *Boondocks*. This episode is more of a clever homage to the Peanuts classic, than a parody. The series' main character Huey is asked to be the director of his school's Christmas play—sound familiar? But his creative vision isn't the same as his grandfather's over-simplified version of the holiday, nor is it the multicultural expression of his teacher's lessons. Instead, Huey organizes a sophisticated drama, a Hollywood A-list quality production called "The Adventures of Black Jesus" that the school board eventually wrestles from his uncompromising control. And like Charlie Brown's distracted cast, Huey's peers only want to dance on stage instead of rehearsing as well.

There's also the animated short from Robert Smigel's popular *TV Funhouse* segments that regularly air during

Saturday Night Live. 2002's "Peanuts Christmas" has got to be one of the funniest parodies of the original out there. Smigel's cartoon begins where the children wave their arms, transforming Charlie Brown's little broken tree into the fuller, more decorated, beautiful Christmas tree. Questioning their own miraculous ability, the children use their mysterious arm-waving to transform various elements in their surroundings. They magically turn a broken down vehicle into a sportscar, a homeless man's cardboard sign into a neon advertisement, and a weary crack-whore into a younger licentious prostitute. Wait until you see what happens when the Peanuts kids transform two snow angels.

2007's *Robot Chicken's Half-Assed Christmas Special* contains an outrageous animated segment inspired by the original Peanuts TV special. Instead of warmth and sentimentality, the animators cross into the realm of the absurd. Charlie Brown's adorable little sister, Sally, holds Linus hostage, a la Stephen King's famous book and film, *Misery*. This double-parody ratchets its dark absurdity even higher, as Sally uses Linus' little bald Christmas tree against him. Re-creating the famously cringe-inducing scene from *Misery*, Sally uses the wood trunk and a sledgehammer to hobble the young philosopher, preventing the object of her infatuation from running away.

Perhaps the most subversive parody of the 1965 Christmas classic can be found on Denis Leary's variety special, *Merry F#%$in' Christmas* from 2005. Leary's show presents an animated spoof called "It's Jihad, Farley Towne," in which a character suspiciously resembling Charlie Brown—here called Farley Towne—is unhappy with the true meaning of Christmas and falls under the influence of radical Muslim friend, Linus. In an attempt to express his new radicalism, Farley tries to bomb the holiday pageant. The two boys turn Farley's failed little bomb into a much bigger bomb by wrapping it with Linus' blanket, nurturing it much like the little, broken tree. The bigger bomb detonates and kills them both. Farley and Linus end up in the fiery depths of Hell, and the pessimistic Farley asks the Devil for 72 Red-Headed Girl virgins but instead finds that he gets 72 Marcys. Oh good grief!

Twas the Grinch Before Christmas

The 1999 animated series, *The PJ's,* features an episode entitled "How the Super Stole Christmas," a clear parody of the original Dr. Seuss special. Inner city building superintendent Thurgood Stubbs is angry with his tenants who don't provide the holiday tips he thinks he deserves. So, he signs on to be the neighborhood repo man for the local pawn shop in order to earn enough money to buy his wife her dream gift of a computer. The scenes of Thurgood using his pass key to sneak into his tenants' homes to repossess their items recall scenes from *The Grinch.* But when Thurgood has his inevitable change of heart and attempts to return the pawn shop goods, he is forced to drag the immense bag back to the projects with the help of a street junky named Smokey, in place of Grinch's dog, Max.

Joy to the Weird

Because of the immense popularity of *Rudolph, Charlie Brown,* and *The Grinch,* viewers have developed an appetite for and have come to expect more animated Christmas material every year. However, as tastes have changed over time, we've come to expect our Christmas specials to reflect these changes. Consider the following irreverent, boundary-pushing, and occasionally downright offensive episodes from animated TV series. We'll start with absurd episodes and work our way toward completely subversive stories.

Space Ghost Coast to Coast, the surreal animated spoof of TV talk shows, created its first Christmas show in 1994 with Space Ghost, Zorak and the Council of Doom singing their own versions of several traditional Christmas carols. The 1994 episode featured an absurd interview with comedian Kevin Meaney. However, in subsequent years, the holiday episode became a clip show, substituting different nonsensical interviews with celebrities between the original three carols to create a Christmas show that is as off the wall as the regular episodes. The 2001 "A Space Ghost Christmas" episode included interviews with comedian/musicians Tenacious D (from 2001's "Sweet for Brak" episode), cartoonist Matt Groening (from the 1996 episode "Glen Campbell"), and Rob Zombie and Raven Symone (from 1997's "Piledriver" episode). The Tenacious D interview features a song by band members Jack and Kyle which is obviously dubbed with someone else's poorly performed version of "Good King Wenceslas," comically turning the regular season segment into a holiday installment. In the third interview, Space Ghost welcomes his grandfather who is visiting from Boca Raton over the holidays. The old-timer is a retired wrestler who insists on taunting Rob Zombie and the ten year-old Raven Symone. Even Space Ghost knows the humiliation of embarrassing relatives at holiday time.

The 2001 *Family Guy* episode, "A Very Special Family Guy Freakin' Christmas" pushes all the right buttons in its irreverent take on a typical dysfunctional Griffin family Christmas. A drunken Peter accidently donates all of the family's Christmas gifts to charity, and the dog burns the house down. Lois loses her mind trying to provide holiday cheer for everyone else, and baby Stewie gets to be a riotously funny baby Jesus in the Nativity play. The episode alludes to many other Christmas TV specials and even creates a new one for Peter to obsess over, "KISS Saves Santa" with preposterous guest stars and plotlines. A cool thing about this episode is that KISS band members Gene Simmons, Ace Frehley, Peter Criss and Paul Stanley provide their voices to this ridiculous tribute to holiday specials past.

Crass Kringle

Where some animation exists in an absurd reality all its own, other animated episodes venture further into gross-out humor and crassness. Unimaginative puerile animation abounds, but the following episodes combine a sharp-witted point of view with vulgarity for these provocative Christmas installments.

1993's outrageous *Ren & Stimpy* created the irreverent holiday episode "Son of Stimpy" making fun of the saccharine nostalgia of the inevitable family reunions that fill the story lines of other holiday-themed programs. "Irreverent" doesn't seem to capture the spirit of this episode, also known as "Stimpy's First Fart." One day, Stimpy farts while watching TV but loses track of the one he names "Stinky." He looks everywhere for his lost fart but the little one eludes him. As Christmas draws closer, Stimpy grows even more sentimental for his departed offspring and leaves Ren for a journey to the city to reunite with his missing Stinky. On Christmas, Stimpy returns home to Ren, defeated in his quest for family. But the heart-warming reunion takes place after all, when Stinky comes home in order to share his life with his father and introduce his bride-to-be, a dead fish carcass. I'm wondering, is a marriage between a fart and a fish corpse even legal?

Another low-brow classic "Beavis and Butt-head Do Christmas" reaired throughout the mid-1990s. One of the show's irreverent sketches called "Huh-Huh-Humbug," focuses on Beavis, with the dimwitted teen receiving visits from three Dickensian ghosts that are unable to teach him anything. Another sketch entitled "It's a Miserable Life" focuses on Butt-head, in a very dark retelling of *It's a Wonderful Life.* All of Butt-head's neighbors pray that the destructive teen will "go away" permanently, so his guardian angel, Charlie, is dispatched to make everyone's Christmas wish come true. Unable to do the deed, Charlie requests Butt-head end his own life, offering to show him how much better the world would be if he were no longer around. Of course, Butt-head doesn't learn from his vision—he only observes that his friend Beavis, without his influence, foolishly volunteers at charity work wearing an uncool Winger t-shirt.

Don't miss the porno that Beavis watches, entitled "Ebenezer Screw" with Tiny Johnson and Bob Scratchit.

In 2000, *TV Funhouse,* the combination live-action and animated series that spoofs children's Saturday morning programming, produced the holiday episode "Christmas Day." This funny episode consists of two animated segments and several live-action sequences with the show's host, Doug. The first animated segment, "Christmas with Tingles" is about the magical elf responsible for delivering holiday stress headaches. The second, "The Harlem Globetrotters First Christmas" is an animated short in the style of the 1970's Saturday morning cartoons, with the world famous basketball team competing on the court with Mary and Joseph for the last room at Bethlehem's inn. A live action segment, "Places to Look for Your Christmas Presents" suggests ridiculous possible locations for hidden gifts for children. But the truly bizarre elements of this episode are the live-action portions featuring both the

The black-and-white, stop motion segment entitled "Christmas With Tingles" is actually a satire of the beloved animated 1950s short, ***Hardrock, Coco and Joe: The Three Little Dwarves.***

Anipals and series host, Doug. The Anipals, (or animal puppets if you haven't seen *TV Funhouse*), are filled with curiosity about Doug's Christmas cheer. They tap his spine to drain the cheer and chemically reduce the pink liquid into a concentrated form which they inject to experience their own Christmas psychedelic freak-out. While Doug has temporary paralysis due to the amateur spinal tap, the Anipals, high on cheer, roam the streets of New York City aggressively caroling to tourists. The story culminates at a Nativity pageant of live baby ducks where the Anipals redeem themselves from their cheer abuse, singing "Angels We Have Heard on High." A Christmas psychedelic freak-out from concentrated Christmas cheer—we've all been there, huh?

O Little Town of Blasphemy

Though crude and vulgar humor can provoke and shock viewers, other holiday episodes go even further to capture viewers' attention by deliberately mocking the religious message of the season. The following animated episodes use blasphemy and sacrilegious humor to push boundaries and to put the "outrage" in outrageous.

Sealab 2021 spoofs intolerant religious beliefs about Christmas in the 2002 episode "The Feast of Alvis." In the underwater research facility known as Sealab, it is time for the annual celebration of the Feast of Alvis, an obvious parallel to Christmas. Captain Murphy plans a traditional Alvian celebration, but crew members complain about the offense of a religious holiday celebrated at the expense of their beliefs when only a third of them is Alvian. As an explanation of the Alvian religion, this episode opens with a bizarre western story about the virgin birth of Alvis that took place amidst the pioneers and Native Americans of the historical past. The story loosely resembles the biblical Nativity. Rigidly holding fast to his intolerant plans for the Alvian celebration, Murphy hallucinates an angelic vision of Alvis himself. The Spirit reveals to him the true meaning of the season—it may not be what you expect! In the scene of the pioneer history, don't overlook the settler who is a hilarious dead-ringer for Michael Landon straight out of *Little House on the Prairie*. Additionally, could this reference to Alvis be a distortion of Elvis, as in Elvis Presley, who has his own devout cultural following? How very subversive, indeed.

2007 brought viewers a holiday episode of the series *American Dad!* called "The Most Adequate Christmas Ever." Stan's expectations for the Christmas decorations are too high, and he insists that his family drive to the forest to find another tree. But while chopping down the perfect tree, it falls on him and Stan dies. In the Afterlife, he asks for a second chance to return to Earth, but his trial reveals that his arrogance has led him to a just, deserving death. When Stan learns that his family is still in the forest, stranded and about to freeze to death, he steals a heavenly gun and crashes Jesus' birthday party in Heaven. Holding God hostage, he tries to negotiate a second chance at life in order to save his family. It's rumored that pointing a gun at Jesus will get you put on Santa's naughty list.

Perhaps the most sacrilegious attempt to offend at Christmas is made by the creators of *Moral Orel*—a series which is a parody of the stop motion, faith-based children's series, *Davey and Goliath*. In the 2005 episode, "The Best Christmas Ever!" Reverend Putty gives an anti-abortion sermon in church on Christmas Eve claiming that the birth of Jesus was an unplanned pregnancy. Afterward, he tells young Orel to look for the Second Coming of the new

Messiah. When Orel hears his parents arguing that his little brother was unplanned, the boy assumes his sibling, Shapey, is the new Messiah and the apocalypse is at hand. The End Times seem even more imminent to Orel when his parents fighting causes their break up. The final scene is quite disturbing, as the satire shifts to existential commentary. Young Orel stops on the street to pray, putting his faith in God despite his horrible family Christmas—yet the camera pulls up and back to nothingness, leaving the boy spiritually abandoned. The ending is abrupt, very dark and NOT the expected holiday "happy ending" by any standard. I guarantee you won't quickly forget this episode once you've seen it.

On the Naughty List, for Sure

The following animated series are known to be limitlessly offensive in their typical episodes. So it should be no surprise that their Christmas episodes raise the stakes impossibly higher to be aggressively obnoxious. Such is the case for 2008's "Mr. Grumpy-Pants" episode of the nightmarishly surreal and bizarre *Superjail!* Dressed as Santa Claus, the ever-fleeing prisoner Jacknife is caught stealing medication from a children's cancer ward at a hospital. Jailbot, a robot that retrieves escapees, transforms into a sleigh to return the recidivist Santa to the maximum security prison, Superjail. After Jacknife is returned, a cute little girl emerges from Santa's sack—a patient from the cancer ward. The inmates call her "Sanser," mispronouncing the diagnosis on her plastic hospital wristband, and fall in love with the adorable four year old, reading her storybooks and throwing her a party. Meanwhile, it's the Warden's birthday and he becomes so jealous of the little one's youth, the Evil inside of him emerges and literally sets off to kill her. Jared, the prison's accountant, buys a rejuvenating mystery butter in Chinatown for the Warden's birthday cake. The inmates seize the warden's party, making it a party for Sanser. Everyone who eats the mystery butter-infused birthday cake is transformed into a child, so when the Superjail erupts into its inevitable riot, all of the children/inmates run amok in a bloodbath of violence and carnage! I'm going to go out on a limb here to say that this insane comedy may not be what you imagined Christmas to be. Ever.

As if that's not tasteless enough, the 2006 episode "Rebel With a Claus" of the hillbilly cephalopods, *Squidbillies,* takes Christmas to a new level. While delivering toys, Santa is lured to a shack in Georgia by the promise of milk and cookies. There, he becomes the unwitting hostage of squidbilly Early Cuyler and his kin. Santa is bound and gagged while Early demands an impossible ransom from the North Pole. The elves are quick to act to negotiate with the hillbilly terrorists. However, the most promising attempt to release Santa is the arrival of the Silent Knights, a ninja squad of commando elves disguised as a living Nativity. Unfortunately, their failed rescue attempt ends in gory violence. The local Sheriff is slow to realize what's going on at the Cuyler place, distracted by the offering of free venison from the eight deer carcasses hanging on the front porch. This violent hostage story even contains a bloody reference to the Quentin Tarantino film, *Reservoir Dogs.* Mr. Blonde slices off the policeman's ear; Cuyler takes a straight razor to the bound Santa's beard. However both scenes contain the same pan where the camera makes the identical movement up to a hanging bare lightbulb when the slicing and screaming starts.

But the most jaw-dropping Christmas episodes have to be those from the series notorious for its crude tastelessness, *South Park*. In 1997, the creators of this series popularized a new holiday icon for modern audiences: Mr. Hankey, the Christmas Poo. The yuletide turd becomes a symbol that everyone in the town can embrace without offending their individual religious or family traditions. In 1998's "Merry Christmas, Charlie Manson" the kids go to Eric's grandmother's house for Christmas. Cartman's uncle escapes from prison to join his family—and brings along fellow inmate, Charles Manson! Even funnier, Manson becomes obsessed with feel-good Christmas TV specials, changing his forehead swastika tattoo to a smiley face. In the 2000 episode, the boys make their own animated Christmas special, featuring Mr. Hankey and his poo family, to inspire the other residents of South Park with the gift-giving spirit of the holiday.

*Perhaps this **South Park** episode was inspired by an offhand comment made by Eliot Loudermilk, the network exec played by Bobcat Goldthwait, in the 1988 movie, **Scrooged**, when he suggests that ratings-grubbing, Frank Cross, played by Bill Murray, should create a TV Christmas special featuring the Manson family.*

Then there's 2002's "Red Sleigh Down" inspired by the military story of the film *Black Hawk Down*. Cartman is desperate to get a special toy this Christmas, but he's been too ill-behaved to earn it from Santa so he's motivated to do something so nice it will make up for all his naughtiness. He decides to bring Christmas to the less fortunate in Iraq and enlists Santa's help. However, flying over Baghdad, Santa's sleigh is attacked and shot down. The boys recruit Jesus to go in and rescue the injured Santa, who has been captured and subjected to torture by the Iraqis. When Jesus is shot during the escape attempt, his dying words inspire Santa to follow through and bring Christmas to the Iraqi people. With its inclusion of brutal torture scenes, *South Park* goes for the gritty realism you've probably felt was so sorely lacking in most holiday-themed programs.

Just when you think you've seen it all, there's more.

In 2004's "Woodland Critter Christmas," Stan befriends a group of adorable animals in the forest in need of a star for their Christmas tree. He even helps them by building a shelter and a manger so one of the cuddly creatures can birth her baby in comfort. There's a narrator that guides this story in meter and rhyme, and includes several musical numbers, just like any other adorable, children's Christmas special. However, in the most offensive and insane *South Park* Christmas episode yet, the animals trick Stan into killing a mother mountain lion to facilitate the birth of the Anti-Christ. It seems the Woodland Critters are Satan-worshippers that Stan has unwittingly helped by killing their only predator, the mountain lion. In order to stop Satan's future offspring from being born Stan helps teach the mountain lion's kittens how to perform an abortion. Would you believe that complications arise? Kyle receives an anal abortion preventing him from being host to the Anti-Christ; and Santa is forced to use his shotgun to slaughter the Satanic red-eyed Woodland Critters. In the end, we see that the bizarre story is merely Eric Cartman's homework assignment, which he's reading in front of the class, though it hasn't saved us from watching the entire story unfold. Not surprisingly, this is the last *South Park* Christmas episode to date, which begs the question: where else could the show's creators go from here?

*Before their success with **South Park**, creators Trey Parker and Matt Stone made two animated shorts that have become internet favorites. In 1992's "The Spirit of Christmas: Jesus vs. Frosty" the children ignore warnings about placing the magic hat upon the snowman's head with disastrous results. In 1995's "The Spirit of Christmas: Jesus vs. Santa" both icons of Christmas engage in physical combat until the wisdom of ice skater Brian Boitano brings peace. The brilliance of both shorts is that they, like the South Park episodes, humorously remind us that Christmas is really all about the presents.*

Hidden Gems: And Heaven and Nature Sing

Two overlooked yuletide-themed animated episodes deserve more attention for their bizarre sensibilities.

The first is "A Scooter for Yaksmas" a 1996 holiday episode of *Ren & Stimpy*. The show creatively generates its own holiday replacement for Christmas called

"Yaksmas," including a mythology behind a different gift-bringer named Stinky Weezelteats—known for leaving pre-chewed gum in your shoes and driving a sausage cart across the sky. I'm not making this up! In "A Scooter for Yaksmas," Stimpy hopes to receive the Johnny Future Jet Scooter as a gift. He hangs his long johns on the wall for Stinky Weezelteats to fill with sausages and decorates the home and yard to ensure a visit from the Great One, despite the fact that Ren doesn't believe in the Yaksmas hooey. On Yaksmas morning, Ren and Stimpy exchange gifts: Ren receives exactly what he asked for—a jewel encrusted Queen of England statue. But there's no scooter for Stimpy. He finds himself pushed to extremes—will that crazy cat ever get his scooter?

My favorite animated holiday episode is an installment from one of the strangest shows ever, *Tom Goes to the Mayor,* called "Rats Off To Ya!" from 2004. Tom wants to sell t-shirts that say "Rats Off to Ya!" to earn money for his Christmas shopping. He's excited that his plan is approved by the mayor. But his kiosk at the mall is robbed while he's using the restroom and his t-shirt idea and design are pirated by another store, Jesters, run by Croeche (voiced by Jeff Garlin). Jesters turns it into a wildly popular catch-phrase and the must-have holiday item of the season in Jefferton. *TGTTM* swings from the mundane, to the surreal, to the profane, in a rhythm all its own. If you haven't seen this show, its unique animation style must be seen to be appreciated. There's no attempt at producing smooth and flowing movement of the image, instead manipulated xeroxes of photos are used to animate the characters. This style seems remarkably appropriate to express the do-it-yourself attitude of the ever-industrious Tom.

Here are three wildly creative, yet family-friendly animated holiday stories. Perhaps one of the most original and inventive Christmas episodes of an animated series is from Cartoon Network's food-themed series, *Chowder,* entitled "Hey, Hey It's Knishmas!" In Marzipan City, young Chowder has his heart set on getting an electric broccoli trimmer for Knishmas this year. He even sits on Knish Krinkle's lap and tells him so. But if Mung Daal, Chowder's aged boss and chef, isn't able to bake the best schmingerbread house he's ever made, then Knish Krinkle won't come and give Chowder the gift he wants. With the pressure on, Mung's schmingerbread house keeps collapsing. Not wanting to disappoint Chowder, Mung humbles himself by purchasing a house from another chef. Mung sacrifices his dignity as a chef, but can Chowder have a happy Knishmas if knows his friend's pride is hurt? There's a whole bizarre mythos here for the obvious Santa parallel, Knish Krinkle: he vomits the gift he delivers; he looks like a caterpillar with a blue face and he doesn't talk in words—his tongue hangs out and he "blechs". I know it sounds vulgar, but it's actually quite innocent and charming. This adorable episode must be seen to be believed!

Another animated surprise is 1974's *The Gift of Winter,* employing the voices of talented actors, Gilda Radner and Dan Ackroyd. This delightful television special attempts to explain where snow comes from. Long ago, before snow, people were miserable during the dreary, cold winters. One unhappy city gathered its people to make a formal complaint to the Ministry of Winter. City residents Goodly, Nicely, Bazooey, Rotten and Malicious organize their protest and march off to the distant bureaucratic center to voice their position. Two children in the city, Tender and Small, are asked to stay behind but they sneak off to join the others on their journey. The protesters make the long, treacherous uphill climb to the Ministry of Winter building, but are denied access to lodge their formal complaint due to inefficiencies of the bureaucracy. But the clever people find the Minister and tell him how unhappy they are with winter. The intimidating, gruff Minister is unreceptive to their complaints until he overhears Small and Tender talking compassionately about how sad and lonely it must be to be a cog in the wheel of this inhumane system. The Minister of Winter cries flakes of snow that fall upon the two children and they instantly fall in love with the beauty and fun of it. And, that's how wonderful snow came to be a part of Christmas and winter. This weird and sincere cartoon classic has amazingly original character design and style. It also evokes the familiar 1970s zeitgeist of political movements and people coming together to work towards a solution to systemic problems. Finding this cult classic is well worth the search.

And, the 1991 British-made children's special *Father Christmas,* based on the well-known author Raymond Briggs' book, gives us an amusing look at the life of Father Christmas the other 364 days of the year when he's not delivering toys. However, this animated depiction of the familiar myth may present itself as more human than expected: Santa overindulges in food while on vacation in France and gets diarrhea; he gets drunk in Scotland, and he goes to Las Vegas to enjoy the sun, gambling, and showgirls. He's even human enough to steal the hotel's towels! This story expands the image of the saintly Father Christmas, depicting him less like a supernatural being on a pedestal and more like one of us. However, it remains modest enough for children.

MYOM:
Animated Ebenezers

Many anticipate the 2009 release of yet another animated retelling of Charles Dickens' *A Christmas Carol*—this time voiced by the multi-talented Jim Carrey. This may be a good time to reflect on just a few, remarkable earlier animated versions to consider how well the new one stands up. I'm skipping over: *Mr. Magoo's Christmas Carol, Walt Disney's* "A Mickey's Christmas Carol," *Fat Albert's Christmas Special, Gumby's* "A Scrooge is Loose," *Rankin/Bass' The Stingiest Man in Town, Bug's Bunny's Looney Christmas Tales, A Flintstone's Christmas Carol,* and *Jetson's Christmas Carol,* just to name a few. Now let us compare three especially unique animated versions of Dickens' classic.

***Photo**: Stan with the seemingly innocuous critters in **South Park's** "Woodland Critter Christmas" (2004).*

Comedy Central/ Photofest

In the 2006 episode of *American Dad!* entitled "The Best Christmas Story Never," Stan is frustrated that everyone doesn't celebrate the holidays the way he does, and decides to give up on Christmas. The Ghost of Christmas Past, voiced by Lisa Kudrow, visits Stan in his sleep, taking him back to Christmas 1970, but he ditches the ghost for his own agenda. Through a series of loose connections, Stan blames "Hanoi Jane" Fonda for the loss of Christmas spirit in America as well as his own disillusionment. His agenda is to find Fonda in 1970 to assassinate her and prevent her influence on American culture. His wife Francine helps the Ghost of Christmas Past retrieve Stan but his impact on the past has already changed the future: America has become a part of Communist Russia. The Ghost and Stan have to time travel again to 1970 to fix the past, including the impossible task of re-shooting Scorsese's masterpiece, *Taxi Driver*.

A similar time travel-theme is involved in the holiday episode of the animated series, known for its parody of buddy cop TV shows, called *Stroker and Hoop*. In the 2005 installment called, "I Saw Stroker Killing Santa Claus a.k.a. A Cold, Dead, White Christmas," Stroker is at the mall when he witnesses the store Santa being attacked and injected with a deadly poison. Stroker finds a winning lottery ticket at the crime scene and selfishly decides to go skiing at a resort instead of hunting down the mall Santa's attacker. The talking vehicle, C.A.R.R., believes the dying mall Santa is the real Santa but is unable to transport him back to the North Pole in time. So C.A.R.R. tries to save Christmas by hitching his bumper to the reindeer and attempting to deliver Santa's toys. In the meantime, Stroker is visited by three ghosts of Christmas, showing him his past, present and future. Eventually Stroker saves the day by recognizing that his Ghost of Christmas Past was Santa's vicious attacker and that the three ghosts were just trying to cover up their time-traveling lottery scam. Seriously.

And stretching the Dickens' reference even further is the 2000 episode of *Aqua Teen Hunger Force*, entitled "Cybernetic Ghost of Christmas Past From the Future." The Hunger Force's next door neighbor, Carl, is visited by a robot calling himself the Ghost of Christmas Past. The robot ghost recounts the legend behind the ancient Christmas celebration which involves Sir Santa, an ape-like creature that made toys for chimps from dinosaur bones. According to his story, the elves are beings from another galaxy enslaved by Sir Santa Ape, who exploits their advanced technology for building toys. The robot claims that Carl's house is the ancient location of Santa's first workshop and the sacred burial ground of the alien elves. This explains why Carl's haunted pool is filled with blood and his shower only flows with the red stuff: Carl must have angered the elf spirits. Disturbed by the supernatural goings-on, Carl moves in next door with the Hunger Force, even selling his house to rocker Glenn Danzig who likes the flowing elfin blood. Even though the details vary from the original nineteenth century transcript, I'm willing to bet this episode of *Aqua Teen Hunger Force* captures the spirit of what Dickens was trying to express so many Christmases ago.

*Look for Carl's vision of his Christmas Past: as a child he received a soiled carpet sample as a gift from under the family Christmas tree. Many may recognize this reference to a soiled carpet sample gift from a 1995 Christmas episode of **The Simpsons** entitled "Marge Be Not Proud" in which Bart imagines what Christmas would be like in juvenile hall. An incarcerated Bart fears he would be lucky to receive a soiled wig while fellow delinquent Nelson Muntz would receive a book of carpet samples.*

MYOM: THE 12 DAYS OF CULT TV CHRISTMAS—Part 2

6. You Are Entering the Christmas Zone. An annual favorite holiday episode, *The Twilight Zone*'s "The Night of the Meek," from 1960, sees a softhearted department store Santa, played by Art Carney, given the ability to make Christmas wishes come true when he finds a magical sack. But have you seen the remake of the same episode from the 1985 reincarnation of the series called *The New Twilight Zone*? The second version stars Richard Mulligan in the lead role and is directed by veteran film director Martha Coolidge.

5. What the Heck IS a Sugarplum? The animated TV series based on the cult comic, *The Tick* includes a 1995 holiday episode called "The Tick Loves Santa." In it the Tick finds himself confronting a bank-robbing Santa Claus. Making matters worse, this Santa can produce equally malicious copies of himself if he is electrocuted. He begins to flood the city with evil Santas after zapping himself in the city's hydroelectric dam. Absurdly, the Tick is hesitant to battle Santa Claus, the very spirit of Christmas!

4. The Names Have Been Changed to Protect the Innocent. In 1953's Christmas episode of *Dragnet*, "The Big Little Jesus," the self-righteously uptight Sgt. Joe Friday and his partner investigate the theft of a baby Jesus figurine stolen from a church's Nativity display. In 1967, with the color revival of the series, this same episode is remade under the title, "The Christmas Story." Look for actor Barry Williams in one of his pre-*Brady Bunch* roles, playing the second altar boy questioned by the police, and actor/jazz pianist Bobby Troup playing the theft's main suspect. One of Troup's many achievements is that he penned the classic song "Route 66." If this isn't enough awesomeness, check out the 1989 holiday episode of *MacGyver*, entitled "The Madonna" which "borrows" this classic *Dragnet* story line.

3. Angels We Have Heard in High School. In the 1994 holiday episode of the teen melodrama, *My So-Called Life,* entitled "So-Called Angels," Angela, wrestling as always with her own teenage, angst-ridden internal dialogue, is affected by an otherworldly homeless girl in an abandoned building. The actress portraying this ethereal character is none other than singer/songwriter, Juliana Hatfield, the former member of the indie rock group Blake Babies, as well as a successful solo artist.

Another teen show with a cult following is *Square Pegs* from the 1980s, a show with plenty of corresponding '80s attitude and popular culture references. In the 1982 two-part holiday episodes, "A Child's Christmas in Weemawee," Lauren's quest for popularity includes a schedule and a map for crashing all the socially important holiday parties over school break, including Vinnie's legendary New Year's Eve bash. But best friend Patty's participation comes into question when her divorced father, played by former *Leave It to Beaver* co-star, Tony Dow, insists that she spend the holiday ice fishing with him. Lauren volunteers to be Santa in the school pageant so she can overhear the popular kids talking about additional exclusive Christmas parties, while Muffy organizes children carolers dressed in international costumes to roam the halls raising money for the class charity. In Part 2, Patty wants a pair of contact lenses for Christmas but her father still sees her as a little girl—not a young woman. Eventually she makes him understand, and she's able to attend the class pageant where she tells the story of the ninth reindeer, played by New Waver Johnny Slash. The class members exchange Secret Santa gifts and Patty and LaDonna harmonize for a cool performance of "Deck the Halls." Don't forget that *Sex and the City*'s Sarah Jessica Parker stars in this 1980s series as the confused teenager, Patty, as does fellow 1980s movie actress Jamie Gertz, playing the role of class busybody, Muffy. Series creator (and former *SNL* writer) Anne

The rock band The Waitresses performed the theme song to the cult show ***Square Pegs*** *as well as the classic New Wave Christmas song "Christmas Wrapping."*

Beatts appears in a cameo role as the international children's choir leader.

2. Wakko Nipping at Your Nose. *Animaniacs* is one of the few clever and irreverent children's animated programs that also has a significant adult following because it is filled with pop culture references. The original run of the series had many silly Christmas-themed segments. Here are three of the best: "Noel" from 1996, "Little Drummer Warners" from 1993 and "The Great Wakkorotti: The Holiday Concert" also from 1993. "Noel" is the familiar Christmas song, performed by the three Warners, with new lyrics loaded with puns on the word "noel." "Little Drummer Warners" is the rare segment that lacks the over-the-top silliness of most of the other *Animaniacs* cartoons. Instead, the three Warners appear as the three shepherds of the Nativity story and they sing mostly traditional Christmas carols. Eventually, they offer the baby Jesus their gift of music: a swing jazz arrangement of "The Little Drummer Boy." "The Great Wakkorotti: The Holiday Concert" is the reoccurring musical segment where Wakko imitates the great tenor, Luciano Pavarotti, only instead of singing, he belches the holiday song "Jingle Bells."

Fans will want to watch the animated spin-off series' 1995 holiday episode too, "A Pinky and the Brain Christmas," where Brain once again pursues his schemes for world domination. This time he invents a Noodle Noggin doll through which he can hypnotize the entire world. He decides to take advantage of the mass production available at the North Pole to manufacture his toy and have Santa deliver it. Just when his scheme is about to work, Brain is overcome by the generous sentiment in Pinky's letter to Santa, and the hypnotic message he sends all over the world is for everyone to have a Merry Christmas.

1. Santa like you've never imagined. 2005 offered two installments of an anime that challenged the mythos of the western Christmas gift-bringer in *My Santa!* and its sequel, *My Santa: Merry Christmas*

Once More. In the first episode, we are introduced to a solitary boy named Santa—so named because he was born on Christmas Eve. He's sad because he is constantly teased for his unusual name. Santa is lonely and he's never able to spend the cheery holiday with his parents who are always away working. At the mall, he meets a gawky teenage girl named Mai who claims to be Santa Claus and who wants to make him happy. Though she hasn't finished all her Claus training, when she experiences the fullness of her magic, Mai transforms into a blonde, voluptuous, woman and her stuffed animal friend, Pedro, becomes an enormous, live reindeer. This stylized romance ends with Santa believing that Mai really is Santa Claus when he accompanies her delivering gifts on Christmas Eve and he has the best birthday of his life. The second installment continues the romance for a full year under the stipulation that Mai must return by Christmas Eve to continue her Santa education. This mature, gender-bending revision of our familiar Man in the Red Suit is nothing like what Clement Moore ever described!

Both episodes take their inspiration from the Ken Akamatsu manga entitled ***Itsudatte My Santa!*** *which translates to* ***Always My Santa***. *Akamatsu also created the popular manga,* ***Love Hina***.

It Was a Dark & Stormy Christmas

Not everyone shares the world view that Christmas shows should be magical, showing us that miracles always happen when you need them most, and that Christmas is the happiest time of the year. Some of us with a slightly bent sense of humor and perspective on life appreciate a dark, even ironic holiday tale rather than the more innocent, family-friendly Pollyanna standards to which others cling.

Over the years, Christmas has become synonymous with "hope." Darker attitudes seem subversive and uncomfortably contradict the spirit of the season for many viewers. But it is this contrast of feelings and expectations that leads to some of the more thrilling and outrageous TV Christmas experiences.

Two Lords A-leaping

Dark themes in traditional Christmas material are not new or even rare. Great depths of gloom are expressed in the most traditional and mainstream of all holiday films, Frank Capra's 1946 film *It's A Wonderful Life*. Frustrated businessman, George Bailey is so distraught by his money troubles that he contemplates his own suicide at the railing of a frozen bridge. An angel named Clarence spends the rest of the movie trying to convince George that his family and friends would be better off with him alive rather than dead! How very dark indeed.

America's favorite film director made another dark Christmas film about a suicidal jumper that many argue is a better film than the ubiquitous Jimmy Stewart picture: the 1941 film, *Meet John Doe,* starring Gary Cooper and Barbara Stanwyck. In this complicated, emotional roller coaster of a plot, a newspaper writer, Mitchell (Stanwyck) is about to lose her job, so she sparks local readers' interest by writing a fake letter to the editor claiming to be an anonymous man so disgusted with the current state of humanity that he threatens to commit suicide on Christmas Eve. The fictional letter strikes a chord with the public and Mitchell is granted a chance to keep her job. She's given a column to continue to spread the fictional man's opinions and folksy wisdom. However, she must now hire an actual man (Cooper) to play her phony John Doe for the public. A grassroots movement quickly arises, as Mitchell's column is picked up nationally, and the initial cynicism of John Doe is replaced with idealism, as he begins to encourage people to make the world a better, friendlier place. Unfortunately, John Doe's newfound political movement is corrupted by an ambitious businessman who wants to abuse Doe's power for his own political gain, thus ending the groundswell of idealism that swept the country. The final scene of the movie takes place on the roof of the local government building on Christmas Eve, with John Doe prepared to make good on his original promise to commit suicide because of the depressing condition of modern society.

The classic holiday song "Have Yourself a Merry Little Christmas" was written for Judy Garland to sing in the 1944 movie ***Meet Me in St. Louis****. The original lyrics were much darker, reflecting the sadness of the scene within the movie where it was to be sung. However, more hopeful lyrics were written before the song was recorded. Later recordings brightened the songs lyrics even more. Could this song have become the holiday anthem that it is if the original dark lyrics had prevailed?*

What makes this film even darker than Capra's later film is that *It's A Wonderful Life* considers only George Bailey's life and the circumstances in Bedford Falls, while *Meet*

John Doe extends its cynical criticism of humanity to the entire country, making it a grander message with potentially more consequence. It's not merely about one person's meaning in life but about what we as a society have become. When John Doe's idealism spreads like wildfire across the United States with John Doe Societies forming all over and ordinary citizens giving testimony to transforming their lives for the better, the film embraces this good will wholeheartedly. When the social movement is crushed and destroyed by the business tycoon who can't exploit it for his own gain, film viewers who were raised up by the film's idealism are dropped to tremendous emotional lows by the film's destructive twist. In the end, viewers are on the edge of their seats to see what, if anything, will keep John Doe from jumping on that Christmas Eve.

Photo*: Gary Cooper and Barbara Stanwyck in Frank Capra's* ***Meet John Doe*** *(1941).*

Warner Bros/ Photofest

The Saddest Christmases Ever

Find yourself feeling moody at holiday time? Sometimes the easiest thing to do is pop in a video of 1988's irreverent *Scrooged* or 1994's *The Ref*—both are dark, comical holiday films with attitude and edge. But they are also fairly traditional and thus predictable. However, there are other, lesser known holiday films to blow your mind, even for the most jaded Christmas TV junky.

I'll start with one that might be familiar to film students. This melancholy favorite is the critically acclaimed, masterpiece of Canadian cinema, 1971's *Mon Oncle Antoine,* which depicts a bittersweet, coming-of-age story for young Benoit in a small Quebec mining town of the 1940s. The story takes place over Christmas Eve as the teenager detachedly witnesses the lives around him. Unlike other teens, Benoit silently looks on to the adult world with dread rather than excitement or eagerness. The general store where he works premieres their holiday store window display. The condescending mining boss hands out free stockings to his workers from a sleigh. And, Benoit's teenage co-worker's exploitative father arrives to collect her wages. The climax of the story is when Benoit accompanies his boss, Antoine, on a long journey in a sleigh during a blizzard to retrieve the body of a recently deceased teenager on Christmas Eve. This film has smothering ennui, an emotion not often evoked in Christmas movies. Too often holiday films hamfist heightened, predictable emotions, forcing tears and then joy within a feature's length, while *Mon Oncle Antoine* is a brilliant reminder of the subtlety of emotion and complexity of human experiences even at Christmas time.

If a truly sad movie is what you crave, then be sure to have a full box of tissues on hand for 1957's *All Mine to Give.* The movie is also known by the revealing title, *The Day*

They Gave the Babies Away—which pretty much sums it up. Touted as a true story, a nineteenth century Scotch immigrant family loses its parents to disease, forcing Robbie, the oldest of the six young children, to find homes for his younger siblings as his dying mother wished. Not wanting to be placed in a state workhouse for orphans, Robbie goes door-to-door on Christmas day, asking families to take in one of his siblings, who he has pulled there on a sled. This isn't just another emotional Christmas movie, it's one of the saddest movies ever. One can only surmise the filmmaker's intent to create a story of hope and a future for the successful adoptions, but it's a hard message to gather after so much sadness. It's just heartbreaking to see young Robbie forcing his little sisters onto the sled in order to find them decent homes. When his young brother, Kirk, cries and doesn't want to be separated from his older brother, it's just wretched. In the final scene, Robbie doesn't even accept a home for himself, the twelve year-old just walks off into the snowy landscape to find a job in a lumber camp! Sniff!

Crime Doesn't Stop at Christmas

One of the most unusual Christmas movies is also one of the most unusual examples of *film noir*, 1947's *Lady in the Lake*. This well-known *film noir* is an adaptation of a Raymond Chandler novel, featuring Robert Montgomery as his hardboiled private detective Phillip Marlowe. The film's story unfolds with the point of view of the camera in first person—audiences watch from the perspective of the detective himself and the characters within the story look and talk directly into the camera. In a unique interactive film experience, the audience sees what the detective sees. The mystery story focuses on a search for a pulp magazine publisher's missing wife. It takes place at Christmas and there are several holiday scenes. However, the holiday elements are most often used ironically, such as the scene in which Marlowe confronts a dangerous suspect at his wreath-decorated apartment door. For the pessimistic Marlowe, the happy holiday is just one more dark day filled with treachery. His fatalistic *film noir* world stands in stark contrast with the friendliness and the hopefulness of the yuletide season. The film opens with festive Christmas carols, that can be heard throughout the picture—ironically, they evoke a constant reminder of the doom awaiting our characters. This *film noir* has the typical elements of a corrupt cop and a deadly *femme fatale*, but there is one surprising element as well. The cynical, sardonic Marlowe experiences a happy ending—a requisite in any other holiday film—but sadly out of place and against expectation in a *film noir*.

Twisted TV Tales

There are certain TV series that regularly tell dark, twisted tales and continue to do so at Christmas as well. *Alfred Hitchcock Presents* is one such program, boasting several warped holiday installments. A favorite episode, personally directed by the Master of Suspense himself, is 1956's "Back for Christmas." A British couple, Herbert and Hermione Carpenter, are planning a long trip to the States, promising their friends that they will be "back for Christmas." But after they say their goodbyes and close up the house, Herbert enacts his well thought-out plan: he murders his wife and buries her body under their cellar floor. Once in America, Herbert continues his clever deception, writing letters to their friends back home announcing their new permanent residence in Los Angeles. However, even though she's dead, Hermione still finds a way to bring Herbert "back for Christmas", when he receives a bill in the mail from remodelers in England commissioned by his late wife to excavate the cellar floor. Completists should know that this episode is based on a story written by John Collier, and was adapted again in 1979 for an episode with the same title on the British series Roald Dahl's *Tales of the Unexpected.*

Another series known for its dark themes, even at Christmas time, is the cynical comedy *Married...With Children*. Perhaps the darkest is the first season's "You Better Watch Out" from 1987. The nearby Lakeside Mall has a Christmas publicity stunt that goes horribly wrong—a parachuting Santa Claus falls out of the sky and plummets to his death in the Bundy's backyard. Though the neighborhood children need emotional comfort, Kelly and Bud aren't as sensitive. It becomes a Christmas to remember only when the Bundys find the dead Santa's bag full of mall gift certificates. This will be a rare Christmas with presents for the Bundys.

The series' third season holiday episode, "It's a Bundyful Life, Part 2" is also comically demented. Al Bundy comes home without the money from his Christmas Club account and his family isn't very forgiving. After regretting that he was ever born, Al is visited by his guardian angel (played by Sam Kinison) who shows him what his family's lives would be like without him: Peg becomes a June Cleaver-type while Bud and Kelly are intelligent and squeaky clean. Peg's new husband, Norman Jablonsky is a hardworking professional, and a loving husband and father. Of course, Al can't stand how happy the Jablonskys are without him so he insists that his guardian angel return him back to his former life. Sam Kinison, the late, great stand-up comedian is perfectly cast as Al's screaming, miserable guardian angel in search of earning his own wings.

'Tis the Season to Be Jolly

It is one thing for a show with a point of view as cynical as *Married... With Children* to create a dark holiday episode. It is even more shocking to see a dark Christmas episode from a program that usually doesn't embrace such an attitude. For instance, in the 1976 episode of *Laverne & Shirley* entitled "Oh Hear The Angels' Voices" the gang from the Pizza Bowl are asked to perform for the sick over Christmas. However, they don't know until they arrive that they've been asked to entertain at a mental hospital. After some awkward moments around the patients, Shirley, Laverne and friends get into the spirit of the holiday and help the people in the ward celebrate. And, the 1995 episode, "Do You Fear What I Fear?" from Ellen DeGeneres' first hit sitcom, *Ellen,* finds her morose at Christmas. Ellen is shocked to receive a cemetery plot as her Christmas gift from her very traditional parents. She becomes obsessed with death and dying, ending up at the graveyard with her friends on Christmas Eve. As her friends and bookstore co-workers decorate the tombstones and an angel statue near Ellen's plot, they contemplate whether her life is meaningful and which Christmas TV special is best.

Another remarkably twisted episode comes from an unlikely source: *The Jack Benny Show*. The fact that it comes from such a mainstream, classic program, makes it all the more subversive. In it, Jack goes to the department store to buy his Christmas presents. He roams between the departments, buying an expensive leather wallet for Don Wilson, a watch for Mary Livingston, and lingerie for his sister. As Jack wanders around shopping, he repeatedly returns to the sales clerk, played by Mel Blanc, at the wallet counter to rewrite the card on Don Wilson's gift. All the changes demanded by Jack hilariously fray the nerves of the eager-

Jack Benny Show regular, Mel Blanc, was the famous voice behind Warner Brothers' Looney Tunes characters, including, Bugs Bunny.

to-please sales clerk and drive him further toward the edge. In the end, the sales clerk takes his own life only to have Jack step over his body in order to give himself a refund and return Wilson's gift!

King of the Hill produced an incredible black comedy Christmas installment with the frightening and macabre, 2004 episode "Ms. Wakefield." An elderly stranger, Ms. Wakefield visits the Hill home, explaining that years before, she used to live in their house. The Hill family welcomes her inside and extends to her warm hospitality. That is, until Ms. Wakefield reveals that she has no intention of leaving—she wants to die in their house! On numerous occasions Hank has to physically eject the determined old woman, even calling the police to charge her with trespassing. Frighteningly, she keeps breaking into their home and terrorizing the family with the promise that she will die soon enough. At Hank's Christmas party, his neighbors and friends convince him to stop forcing her to leave, even though her presence at the party leaves everyone feeling awkward. This episode is made even creepier by the fact that the character, Ms. Wakefield is recognizably voiced by Marian Ross, the same actress known for playing the warmhearted mother, Mrs. Cunningham on the long running *Happy Days* series.

One of the darkest comedic holiday episodes of *King of the Hill* is 1998's "Pretty, Pretty Dresses." Bill struggles with depression and suicide at Christmas, this marking seven years since his wife Lenore left him. Hank can't give up on his former football team member and even organizes the neighbors into a suicide watch schedule. In his desperation to have his ex-wife return to him, Bill loses his grip on reality and becomes "Lenore"—wearing her old clothes, speaking in her voice and frightening Hank's confused holiday party guests. In a touching moment of compassion, Hank painfully dons a dress in order to act out his own version of "Lenore," giving Bill one last chance to confront the woman who hurt him so deeply. Few shows' story lines go as far as "Pretty, Pretty Dresses" to portray mental breakdown and suicide at the holidays.

Perhaps the darkest holiday chapter is the 1952 episode of the police procedural, *Dragnet*, entitled ".22 Rifle for Christmas." Just before Christmas, Sgt. Friday investigates the heartbreaking case of a missing nine year-old boy. Eventually the young boy returns home unharmed but reveals that he took what was to be his Christmas present, a Winchester rifle, from under the Christmas tree, and accidentally shot his best friend to death. With the introduction, "Ladies and Gentlemen, the story you are about

***Photo**: Grandpa Squirrel and his grand-squirrels in Hugh Harmon's **Peace On Earth** (1939).*

MGM/Photofest

to see is true," viewers may recognize that reality is sometimes far more horrible than fiction. And your mother was only worried about you shooting out your eye!

Nuclear Winter Wonderland

Most people tend to view Christmas as a time to reflect on peace and serenity—a time to lay down arms if possible and remember our human commonalities. It is with this intent that certain creative people have produced Christmas visual media to remind us of these sentiments, while others have generated more extreme messages—not just antiwar content but disturbingly dark, out-and-out warnings about post-apocalyptic Christmases of our future. It is to these that we turn out attention.

In 1939, legendary animator, Hugh Harmon created *Peace on Earth,* a stunning antiwar MGM cartoon in Technicolor, made with the foreboding of devastating war in Europe at that time. This gorgeous-looking cartoon depicts a post-apocalyptic society where humans have been killed off, but the animals have rebuilt civilization for themselves. They live amongst the remains of the now obsolete and abandoned human-built war machinery in peace and cooperation. A grandfather squirrel shares a bedtime story with his young on Christmas Eve about how humans monstrously died out because of their thirst for war. The animals rejoice that such horrible creatures no longer exist on Earth and vow to learn from their mistakes and to abide by the rules they find in the good book in a crumbling church. The World War II imagery in this cautionary tale is unmistakable and pretty convincingly scary.

Another version of this cartoon was made in 1955 entitled, *Good Will to Men,* by William Hanna and Joseph Barbera, in Cinemascope, also for MGM. Here, a mouse music director instructs his choirboys about how humans killed themselves off. He explains how their wars became more and more technologically advanced with the apparent purpose to kill as many humans as efficiently possible, until they succeeded. The remaining animals on the planet take lessons from a discarded Bible, the book of rules they refer to in an old church—with special emphasis on "thou shalt not kill" and "love thy neighbor"—and now live peacefully. This update of the earlier tale includes a clear enumeration of killing technology and the advancement of war as well as scenes of nuclear war. Like the 1939 version, this cartoon was also nominated for an Academy Award.

1964 offered a made-for-TV movie version of Dickens' familiar ghostly tale entitled *Carol for Another Christmas* with an extraordinary cast, including Sterling Hayden, Ben Gazzara, Steve Lawrence, Peter Sellers, Eva Marie Saint and Britt Ekland among others. Many cult TV fans have heard of this hard-to-find movie because it was written by TV visionary, Rod Serling. Though I've never seen it, this extreme film is the stuff of TV legend. This political message film retells *A Christmas Carol*. Here the miserly Scrooge character is replaced with an isolationist, politically conservative character named Daniel Grudge, played by Hayden. The story is told against the backdrop of an escalating Vietnam War/anti-Communist America. Grudge must learn his moral lesson—not about charity and responsibility to the poor as Dickens would call for—but instead about the need for world peace, the cause of the United Nations and continued diplomacy as a means to avoiding war. Marked by his son Marley's death in a foreign war, Grudge is converted after meeting his three ghosts. The Ghost of Christmas Past is a WWI soldier reminding him how isolationism didn't work then either.

The Ghost of Christmas Present shows Grudge the hunger and pain of those in political refugee camps. And the Ghost of Christmas Future shows Grudge the consequences of his isolationism: a devastated and savage society in a post-apocalyptic world following a nuclear war. Critics have referred to this difficult to find film as propaganda and "a product of its times" but this only makes it seem even more intriguing. Come on, it's Rod Serling—how bad could it be?

The 1969 family film *The Christmas Tree* starring William Holden, shares a dark, intensely personal story of the consequences of living in the atomic age. While vacationing, ten year-old Pascal receives a lethal exposure to radiation when a secret airplane carrying an atomic bomb crashes nearby. Laurent Segur (Holden) learns that his young son has only months to live and vows to make the most of Pascal's remaining time—going so far as to stage a dramatic theft of two wolves, Pascal's favorite animal, from the Paris Zoo. On Christmas Eve, the boy has grown so weak, he is found dying under the decorated tree as his wolves howl. This French-made family film is much darker than most other holiday films, as Segur continually winces at the sound of jets flying overhead, reminding him of the ongoing atomic threat.

Woops!, a short-lived TV sitcom with an unusual premise aired in the fall of 1992 before being canceled. It tells the story of six survivors of a nuclear war who lived and worked together after Armageddon—a sort of bizarre, modern-day *Gilligan's Island*. Did I mention that it's a comedy? Of interest here is the unbelievable holiday episode entitled, "Say It Ain't So, Santa" in which the survivors discover that Santa Claus has also survived the nuclear blast. However, he is consumed with tremendous guilt. Santa explains how he pulled the bomb shelter door tightly behind him on that fateful day, inadvertently locking Mrs. Claus and the reindeer out! Later Santa comes to recognize that he has lost the ability to open doors—remember this is the man that only enters homes by way of the chimney—and he's relieved of feeling like their deaths were his fault. However, it is little consolation to the audience, having been dragged to such depths in the previous 30 minutes of the episode. Though this story seems cynical enough to fit right in with some of the *Adult Swim* series made more recently, what seems more inappropriate is that the writers attempted a "happy ending" to this dark episode, with Santa reclaiming his Christmas spirit after coming to terms with his lack of door-opening abilities.

*Who can forget the crazy scene in David Lynch's 1990 film, **Wild At Heart**, featuring the unpredictable actor Crispin Glover. Though the film is not holiday related, Glover's role as Jingle Dell most certainly is. Glover's role occurs as a brief but unforgettable reminiscence by Lula Fortune about her confused cousin, Dell, who wore a Santa suit and wished it was Christmas all year round. Jingle Dell also believed that Christmas was controlled by aliens wearing black rubber gloves who were following him. Just before cousin Dell disappeared, Lula explains, he was found to be placing cockroaches in his underwear and staying up all night making sandwiches. This story, of course, is explained by Lula as an example of someone with "bad ideas."*

To Save Us All From Satan's Power

For many people, Christmas is primarily a religious holiday celebrating the birth of Christ. Despite its blasphemous potential, there are several Christmas stories which include Satan. Certainly when *South Park* and *Space Ghost Coast to Coast* include Satan in their Christmas episodes, it is meant to be offensive and tasteless. However, there are other examples of holiday programming that curiously include the Devil, but without the same crass intent. In Mexican culture, the Devil is often included as a character within Christmas narratives to present a challenge to the goodness of the season, and it is becoming more common in culture north of the border, however shocking it may seem to some TV viewers.

The 1959 movie, made in Mexico and dubbed into English, called simply *Santa Claus* is one such export that now is easily viewable throughout North America. This bizarre film has the Devil ordering his minion, Pitch, to make the people of the world do evil, and so the ridiculous-looking Pitch uses his demonic influence on children as well as throwing obstacles into the path of Santa Claus. Here, Santa lives in a castle in the clouds, instead of the North Pole and surrounds himself with teams of children from all over the world to help him make the toys that he delivers on Christmas. The alchemist Merlin provides Santa with magic powder to make children sleep and a flower to sniff which renders Santa invisible. Santa has creepy anthropomorphized machines that help him spy on the children of the world to determine their niceness or naughtiness. The thin narrative climaxes on Christmas Eve, when Pitch forces Santa up a tree to avoid a barking dog. Santa is trapped in the tree in plain sight because Pitch has removed his invisibility flower. Can he get himself out of this jam and still finish his rounds of toy deliveries?

Another Christmas movie that includes the Devil as a major character is the film *La Pastorela: The Shepherd's Tale* which originally aired as an installment of PBS's *Great Performances* in the 1991 season. In this fable, a teenage girl is hit on the head during her church's Christmas play and she finds herself in a fun-spirited, fantasy story of a Mexican-American version of the Christmas Nativity. As the shepherds journey to see the new born baby, the Devil and his demons place supernatural stumbling blocks along their path to Bethlehem. Throughout her odyssey, the teenager recognizes her family and friends as the characters in the story and she comes to appreciate Christmas as well as her family with renewed enthusiasm. Singer Linda Ronstadt plays the Archangel, comedian Paul Rodriguez plays a demon, Cheech Marin portrays a Wise Man from the East, and Los Lobos provides songs.

Hidden Gems: And Now for Something Completely Different

When looking for Christmas material with a weird twist, consider notorious films that may not be considered Christmas-themed, yet contain a provocative Christmas scene. In *The Life of Brian*, British comedy masters Monty Python create a sacrilegious epic spoof of the life and times of Jesus by telling the story of a man named Brian who is mistaken for the biblical-era messiah. The film starts with the three wise men arriving at the stable with gifts in hand to worship the newborn Savior. Until they realize they are looking for the newborn—next door! Because Brian is also philosophical and questions authority, his life accidentally intersects with Jesus'. This satirical picture is an outrageous substitute for the numerous religious films shown each year at Christmas. Warning: it will leave you singing the closing theme tune until after New Year's!

Perhaps even more outrageous is director, John Water's indelible, lowbrow classic, *Female Trouble,* starring the eye-opening actress, Divine. Here, distraught teen Dawn Davenport runs away and turns to a life of crime when she doesn't receive cha-cha heels for Christmas. Instead she falls under the spell of the depraved owners of the Lipstick Beauty Salon who photograph her criminal acts, calling them "beauty in crime". Her crime spree ultimately leads to her defiant, celebrity death in the electric chair. Divine is at her best here, in hair, fashion, and melodramatic performance. The Christmas scene at the beginning is hilariously over the top: when Dawn doesn't find her cha-cha heels under the tree, she stomps over all the remaining gifts in her fuzzy blue slippers, and knocks the tree down, trapping her mother beneath it. What a Christmas tragedy! Teenagers should reference this movie to their parents to best extort whatever gifts they want most for Christmas. Surely parents don't want to condemn their children to this slippery slope towards a life of crime, inevitably leading to the electric chair, all because of bad Christmas gift-giving.

The dark and unsettling 1955 film *The Night of the Hunter*, starring Robert Mitchum and Shelley Winters, ends at Christmas. After the deranged, murdering minister spends most of the movie hunting down the young children in this highly stylized, film noir suspense chiller, the children survive to spend Christmas in their new home, an orphanage run by a kindly (and plucky) elderly woman, played by Lillian Gish. This notorious film exploits the season of Christmas to bring about some semblance of a happy ending for these poor children, with Gish's character waxing about how God gives his youngest creatures the strength to endure this world's harshest experiences. But few viewers are left feeling optimistic or upbeat with this "happy ending" at Christmas after being terrorized by the relentless madman with the words "love" and "hate" tattooed on his knuckles.

*Don't forget the **SCTV** spoof of Divine featuring John Candy. In the "SCTV Staff Christmas Party" episode from 1981, in the segment with "The Dusty Towne Sexy Holiday Special" legendary performer, Divine, joins Dusty for some lusty Christmas fun. Clearly alluding to her role from Waters' film **Pink Flamingos**, Divine is slid onto the ice inside a playpen surrounded by plastic flamingos. Then she sings "Santa Bring My Baby Back to Me" while ice skating with the Juul Haalmeyer dancers.*

Kids' Christmas: Monsters, Penguins & Chimps, Oh My

The following programs are fantastical and wildly eccentric, yet family-friendly material originally made for children. The first two shows are made-for-TV specials originally crafted half way around the world, in New Zealand. The third is a Castle Films release, sold as holiday material for home projectors, in the days before home video players.

1981's *The Monster's Christmas* is a live-action TV special with imaginative, almost psychedelic characters and costumes, shot on location in Waiotapu Thermal Wonderland, a New Zealand park with rare, geologic features, making the setting seem all the more visually otherworldly. In the story, a little girl on Christmas Eve reads a book about monsters losing their voices due to an evil witch's spell. Upon meeting one of these voiceless monsters, the little girl is filled with compassion and sets out on a long journey to help recover the monsters' voices to allow them to once again sing Christmas carols which they love to do.

Produced and directed by the same creative team, 1982's *Nearly No Christmas* tells the story of Santa Claus' steam engine, Rumbletum, that needs maintenance in order for the elves to produce their toys for Christmas. So Santa travels to the city to earn the money for the necessary repairs. He finds work as a Father Christmas for a department store while Mrs. Claus and the elves enlist the help of penguins to continue the toy manufacturing. This live-action story contains a unique depiction of Santa's North Pole dwelling: an underground, cave-like location. It also calls into question the location of this North Pole, as it relies on the help of penguins which only live in the South Pole. Santa can be seen to ski, boat and jump out of an airplane in this action-filled holiday special. Additionally, *Nearly No Christmas* is filled with elaborate costumes and imaginative surroundings.

My personal favorite wacked-out children's program is the Castle Films release from the 1950s called *Santa Claus' Story*. This black-and-white, ten-minute short sees a young boy and girl, Jackie and Virginia, catch Santa sneaking down their chimney on Christmas Eve. He greets the children and offers to tell them a story of "The Monkeys' Christmas." What follows is edited footage of monkeys in a zoo habitat—fighting over food, swimming in a shallow pool, pulling bananas off the bunch. There are also ridiculous sequences of chimpanzees, with the assistance of their trainers, dressing up for Halloween, and getting ready for bed. There's even a chimp Santa coming down a chimney, and chimp children finding their toys under a Christmas tree. In my favorite sequence, a chimp puts the shaving brush and cream in his mouth instead of accepting the barber's shave. There's not a real story here, just moving images spliced together of monkeys and chimps doing ridiculous things and it's mindlessly funny. It's hard to believe that someone actually spent the time to create this montage in order to sell it as Christmas material. Oh, and someone should tell Santa: chimps are not monkeys—they are apes!

MYOM:
O. Henry's Twisted Ending

Most are familiar with the celebrated author O. Henry and his most famous Christmas short story, "The Gift of the Magi." A young couple in love, Della and Jim, find themselves without enough money at Christmas to afford to give one another a gift. So Della sells her long hair to buy Jim a fob for his pocketwatch, while Jim sells his pocketwatch to buy Della beautiful combs to adorn her long hair. Each now has an impractical, yet heartfelt gift, and experiences the true meaning of generosity. This story has been adapted for television and film numerous times over. However, O. Henry penned another short story, "The Cop and the Anthem" that has become popular at Christmas time and has also been adapted multiple times. This dark tale, like most of O. Henry's stories, also features a surprise, twist ending.

1952's black-and-white feature film *O. Henry's Full House* is a collection of the American humorist's short stories adapted for the screen. It includes five vignettes, the first being "The Cop And The Anthem" directed by Henry Koster and starring Charles Laughton and yes, Marilyn Monroe. The quality of this production is made abundantly clear by the inclusion of the highly regarded American author John Steinbeck as the narrator who introduces each segment. Laughton plays Soapy, the happy-go-lucky hobo who decides that he wants to spend the upcoming winter in a local jail where he will have the assurance of adequate food and shelter until Spring. Not believing in accepting charity, he sets about committing petty crimes trying to capture the attention of a policeman. He steals a man's umbrella but the man had stolen it earlier and won't call a cop. Soapy eats a meal at a fine restaurant and then admits he has no money for the check, but the manager writes the bill off for charity. He breaks a store window, but the police chase another man despite Soapy's pleas that he's the perpetrator. He even propositions a stranger on the street hoping to offend her and cause a stir, but instead his gentlemanly words aren't vulgar enough to offend the prostitute (Marilyn Monroe) and he fails to get arrested. Upset that a decent criminal can't even get arrested anymore, with nowhere to go he roams the city streets until he hears beautiful music coming from inside a church. He finds himself inspired to try to pull himself together, stop being idle and find a job. But it is then that a cop arrests him for loitering in front of the church, and he is sent to prison for vagrancy until Spring. Soapy actually gets what he claimed he wanted all along. However, it's a dark conclusion to an endearing story because the good-natured tramp finally finds within himself the strength to

Charles Laughton is the brilliant actor well remembered for his role as Captain Bligh in the 1935 version of ***Mutiny on the Bounty****. He also directed* ***The Night of the Hunter*** *and was married to Elsa Lanchester, from the movie* ***The Bride of Frankenstein****.*

improve his life. Yet his newfound purpose is squelched by his arrest.

Another retelling of this short story is performed on the Christmas episode of *The Red Skelton Show* by the legendary comedian in the mid-1950s. Skelton's lovable hobo character, Freddie the Freeloader, awakens on a park bench on Christmas Eve with the plan to get arrested so he can spend the holiday and the rest of the winter with a roof over his head and three square meals a day. With this in mind, he tries to get arrested in similar ways. Then, while standing in front of a church, contemplating his next crime, the good-hearted hobo is transformed when he hears a boys choir singing "O Come All Ye Faithful." Freddie decides he wants to change his life, and one of the boys in the choir tells him about a job opportunity at his father's factory. It is then that a policeman walks past and arrests the hope-filled Freddie for vagrancy, taking him away to prison.

Sherwood Schwartz is credited with adapting this short story for ***The Red Skelton Show****. Schwartz is the same genius behind* ***Gilligan's Island*** *and* ***The Brady Bunch****.*

There are two other versions of this O. Henry story adapted for children but neither retains the dark ending. In the charming thirty-minute animated holiday special that features the Pink Panther, 1978's *Pink Christmas*, the lovable cat finds himself homeless, lonely and hungry at Christmas. He desperately makes attempt after attempt to find comfort. When he finally finds a small morsel of food, he shares it with an adorable puppy that is hungry too. *Pink Christmas* was produced by DePatie-Freleng, the same creative team responsible for the original Pink Panther cartoons. The entire story is told without dialogue and features an exceptional jazz soundtrack.

The 1997 animated version of the *Pippi Longstocking* series includes an episode called "Pippi's Christmas" in which she spends her first Christmas on land with her friends at the Winter Carnival. There, she witnesses local ne'er-do-wells, Thunder-Karlsson and Bloom, committing petty crimes for money to stay at a hotel for the holiday. In the spirit of O. Henry's original story, the thieves even try to get arrested so they can spend Christmas in the comfort of jail rather than on the streets. But Pippi rescues them from that bad idea and invites them to her home to share dinner and spend Christmas Eve with her, Mr. Nilsson and Horse.

But perhaps an edgier Christmas story that focuses on reversals of fortune would be the 1983 comedy *Trading Places* starring Eddie Murphy and Dan Ackroyd. Two rich brothers, Randolph and Mortimer Duke, played by veteran actors Ralph Bellamy and Don Ameche, respectively, make a gentlemen's wager concerning the Nature vs. Nurture debate: they take a successful well-bred man, Louis Winthorpe III (Ackroyd) and deprive him of privilege to see if his breeding will allow him to recapture his success. They also take a poor ex-convict, Billy Ray Valentine (Murphy) and set him up with privilege and a job to see if he can adapt and thrive. As a Christmas movie, it plays on the charity aspects of the holiday that are lacking in the two depraved wealthy businessmen who set up their social experiment for their own amusement. But it doesn't end there—Valentine and Winthorpe III learn they are pawns in this great scheme and decide to use their skills to exact revenge and to teach the wealthy brothers a lesson about being the victims of poverty and manipulation. Incidentally, in an earlier scene, the newly down-and-out Winthorpe III is given shelter by a hooker named Ophelia played by Jamie Lee Curtis—easily convincing viewers that living on the streets can't be so bad after all.

Don't miss Senator Al Franken in a minor role in ***Trading Places****. He's got my vote for the wackiest train baggage handler in motion picture history.*

APPENDIX

How to Make Your Own, MAKE YOUR OWN MARATHON

In the spirit of the do-it-yourself-Christmas attitude I've encouraged throughout the book, I challenge you to create your own holiday-themed marathons. Use the resources that you have available to you including online sites, Internet databases, books, and DVD box sets to arrange your own viewing schedule. Follow your own interests. Perhaps you could organize a marathon of Christmas episodes from your favorite television series that has produced several Christmas installments. Or perhaps using The Internet Movie Database, you could research a sequence of holiday-themed materials that your favorite Hollywood star appears in. Feeling more ambitious? You may want to try to collect multiple yuletide episodes that share a common theme. If you really want to impress your friends and family with a complex marathon, try to generate a list of Christmas materials that contains the cast from your favorite non-holiday cult film. Creating interesting MYOMs may not be as easy as one first assumes. However, with a little perseverance you'll be ready for a new career as a television network programming executive. Okay, maybe not, but you'll have a lot of fun in the process. Below is a model of a MYOM of my favorite cult film to use as an example. In addition to the MYOMs throughout the book, you can use this complex example to guide you to generate your own.

MYOM: WHERE'S THE CHRISTMAS, LEBOWSKI?

Fans of the 1998 cult film, *The Big Lebowski,* directed by Joel and Ethan Coen, may want to celebrate the holiday in a style befitting an Achiever. Forget the egg nog and grab a White Russian, sit back and watch your favorite *Lebowski* actors in other projects with a holiday theme.

David Huddleston, known for his role as the wealthy, wheelchair-bound, Jeffrey Lebowski, appears in the TV classic, *The*

Homecoming: A Christmas Story. This is the original 1971 made-for-TV movie about the depression-era Appalachian family that was so well received and highly rated, it inspired the long-running TV series, *The Waltons*. Huddleston's role as Sheriff Bridges has significant screen time, however, it is a large ensemble cast. Huddleston has far more presence playing the title role in the 1985 feature length, children's film, *Santa Claus: The Movie*. This is a far less important film but it serves Huddleston well with a larger role and more screen time.

Sam Elliott, who plays the narrating cowboy character, the Stranger, also stars in the 1989 emotional family movie entitled *Prancer*. Elliot plays a down-on-his-luck farmer and father to the eight year-old girl who wants to return an injured reindeer to Santa. Don't be surprised if you find yourself weeping into your sarsaparilla!

The private dick named Da Fino, played by actor Jon Polito, also appears in a major role in the Christmas episode of *Millennium* entitled "Omerta." While on a holiday vacation, creepy ex-FBI profiler Frank Black finds a former mob hit man, played by Polito, living in the woods with two speechless women who possess the miraculous power to heal. A classic Christmas premise, really.

Jack Kehler, who plays Marty, the landlord with the god-awful dance cycle performance, appears in several holiday episodes but most notably on the 2001 Christmas episode of *Becker* entitled "Ghost of Christmas Presents." The cynical Dr. Becker and his friends at Reggie's diner each decide to answer a child's letter to Santa. Becker puts off his act of charity until the last moment—and ends up stuck in traffic on the bridge to Queens. While stopped in his car, he meets a hitchhiker, played by Kehler, who ends up stealing the child's gift. Later, Becker hears the gift was received by the child anyway. Filled with the holiday spirit, the doctor is left wondering if the hitchhiker was an angel ensuring the gift's delivery.

Leon Russom, the actor who plays the mug-throwing Malibu Police Chief appears in a major role in the 1999 holiday episode of *Diagnosis Murder* entitled "Santa Claude." Here, he plays the kind and gentle Claude a terminal cancer patient, who works at the hospital as the caretaker of the indoor plants that line the hallways. Though Claude is known for playing Santa Claus at the annual Christmas party, his friends discover that he's an escaped convict—jailed for murdering his wife. Lead character, Mark, played by Dick Van Dyke, believes him when he claims he's innocent and sets out to prove it.

Dios Mio, man! Bowling semifinalist and convicted pederast, Jesus Quintana, portrayed brilliantly by actor John Turturro will also appear as the Rat King in the yet to be released film, *The Nutcracker: the Untold Story*, due out in 2009.

Actor Ben Gazzara, who plays porno king Jackie Treehorn, also appears in the 1966 episode "Time and a Half for Christmas Eve" of the TV series *Run for Your Life*. Here, retired lawyer Paul Bryan finds himself alone on Christmas Eve in a strange town until he befriends another loner, a cabbie, played by Ernest Borgnine. The cab driver feels guilty for abandoning a wife and child many years earlier. Gazzara also appears in the rarely seen, 1964 classic, made-for-TV movie *Carol for Another Christmas*, written by Rod Serling. In this pro-United Nations message movie, and revision of the Dickens classic, Gazzara plays the nephew Fred.

There are many holiday-themed programs to choose from to experience John Goodman, the actor who portrays the inimitable Walter Sobchak, at Christmas time. Of course, Goodman appears in each of the four Christmas episodes of the TV series *Roseanne* where he played family patriarch, Dan Conner. The best of these four episodes is 1993's "White Trash Christmas" where Dan and Roseanne take on the neighborhood in a competition to adorn their home for the holiday with the most tacky and tasteless decor. He also provides the voice of Santa in 1998's mostly adequate, animated children's feature, *Rudolph The Red-Nosed Reindeer: The Movie.* He sings an original song for the film, "Santa's Family." He's also in the 1982 animated special, *Frosty Returns,* where he sings "Let There Be Snow." If you've already had more than one White Russian, you may be ready to catch Goodman playing Santa Claus in the 2006 made-for-TV movie, the live-action retelling of the Animagic classic, *The Year Without a Santa Claus.* However, the best Goodman Christmas experience is the twisted holiday episode of *Futurama* entitled, "Xmas Story" where Goodman voices the angry killer robot Santa in this funny animated series. That Santa makes revelers enter a world of pain.

The man who brought the Dude himself to life, actor Jeff Bridges, appears in just one holiday-themed film: made-for-TV's groundbreaking, *Silent Night, Lonely Night* from 1969. This highly rated, TV adaptation of Robert Anderson's Broadway play is an emotional investigation of marriage and fidelity that focuses on two married people who decide to share a brief affair after just meeting. The story takes place in snowy New England over Christmas, and stars Shirley Jones and Lloyd Bridges as the two lovers. Jeff Bridges appears in a small role in a flashback, as the younger version of Lloyd Bridges' character. *Silent Night, Lonely Night* isn't widely available, but it does air on TV occasionally—look out for it to get a glimpse of a decidedly younger Dude—and his real-life father, Lloyd Bridges.

Writing and directing brothers, Joel and Ethan Coen received executive producer credits for the 2003 film *Bad Santa.* And, 1994's The *Hudsucker Proxy,* takes place on New Year's Eve, as the optimistic Norville Barnes, played by Tim Robbins, falls out of the Hudsucker building.

Or, you could just listen to Aimee Mann's 2006 Christmas album *One More Drifter In the Snow,* after listening to Creedence, of course. Singer/musician, Mann played the pancake-eating, female Nihilist who sacrificed her toe to the bungled plot to extort money from the non-Dude Lebowski.

You may want to grab a few In-N-Out burgers and sit back to watch Walter's favorite TV series, the 1965 western, *Branded,* starring squinty-eyed Chuck Connors, in the Christmas episode entitled "A Proud Town." Here, Jason McCord, played by Connors, meets two runaway orphans looking for help after one is accused of shooting a powerful man's son. Promising he'll help them, Jason escorts the two back home to learn that the wealthy Mr. Stoddard wants to force the orphans and their caretaker out of town on Christmas Eve. Warning: like the Dude, you may find yourself singing *Branded's* theme tune, hopefully not while being carted off in the back of a police car.

The author would love to hear about your success stories in creating your own MYOMs. Contact her through the publisher's website with your awesome marathon title.

C

D

E

F

G

H

I

J

K

L

M

N

O

P

Q

R

T

X

Y

Z

About the Author

Joanna Wilson is a *bona fide* pop culture expert who draws upon her background in film and philosophy to create insightful commentary on pop culture of all kinds. She is equally at ease discussing the thoughts of the ancient Greeks on art, Justice, and Virtue as she is in discussing the plot, guest stars, and cultural ramifications of an episode of *Laverne and Shirley*. The unique book you are now holding is her first. At this moment, she is probably hard at work watching yet another obscure Christmas-themed special for her forthcoming book: a comprehensive encyclopedia of Christmas on TV. Look for it next year from 1701 Press!